A Balancing Act

A Balancing Act
Selected and New Poems, 1998-2018

Jim McGarrah

LITERARY PRESS
LAMAR UNIVERSITY

Copyright © Jim McGarrah 2018
All Rights Reserved

ISBN: 978-1-942956-54-9
Library of Congress Control Number: 2018941002

Cover Photo: Bruno Minkley

Lamar University Literary Press
Beaumont, Texas

This book is dedicated to my sister, Sandy, who has been all her life what I have struggled often and failed often to be—a good person.

Recent Poetry from Lamar University Literary Press

Bobby Aldridge, *An Affair of the Stilled Heart*
Michael Baldwin, Lone Star Heart, *Poems of a Life in Texas*
Roberto Bonazzi, *Awakened By Surprise*
David Bowles, *Flower, Song, Dance: Aztec and Mayan Poetry*
Jerry Bradley and Ulf Kirchdorfer, editors, *The Great American Wise Ass Poetry Anthology*
Matthew Brennan, *One Life*
Mark Busby, *Through Our Times*
Paul Christensen, *The Jack of Diamonds is a Hard Card to Play*
Stan Crawford, Resisting Gravity
Chip Dameron, *Waiting for an Etcher*
Glover Davis, *My Cap of Darkness*
William Virgil Davis, *The Bones Poems*
Jeffrey DeLotto, *Voices Writ in Sand*
Chris Ellery, *Elder Tree*
Alan Gann, *That's Entertainment*
Larry Griffin, *Cedar Plums*
Michelle Hartman, *Irony and Irrelevance*
Katherine Hoerth, *Goddess Wears Cowboy Boots*
Michael Jennings, *Crossings: A Record of Travel*
Gretchen Johnson, *A Trip Through Downer, Minnesota*
Ulf Kirchdorfer, *Chewing Green Leaves*
Janet McCann, *The Crone at the Casino*
J. Pittman McGehee, *Extraordinary in the Ordinary*
Laurence Musgrove, *One Kind of Recording*
Godspower Oboido, *Wandering Feet on Pebbled Shores*
Carol Coffee Reposa, *Underground Musicians*
Jan Seale, *The Parkinson Poems*
Steven Schroeder, *the moon, not the finger, pointing*
Glen Sorestad *Hazards of Eden*
Vincent Spina, *The Sumptuous Hills of Gulfport*
W.K. Stratton, *Ranchero Ford/ Dying in Red Dirt Country*
Wally Swist, *Invocation*
Loretta Diane Walker, *Desert Light*
Dan Williams, *Past Purgatory, a Distant Paradise*
Jonas Zdanys, *Three White Horses*

For information on these and other Lamar University Literary Press books go to www.Lamar.edu/literarypress

Acknowledgments

Thanks to Dana Curtis for awarding *Running the Voodoo Down* (Elixir Press, 2003) a book prize.

Thanks to M. Scott Douglas at Main Street Rag for making the book *When the Stars Go Dark* part of his 2008 Select Poetry Series.

Thanks to Jerry Craven at Ink Brush Press for publishing the collection *Breakfast at Denny's* in 2013.

Thanks to Lamar University Literary Press for publishing *The Truth About Mangoes* in 2016.

I would also like to express my gratitude to the numerous magazine and journals that originally published many of these poems over the last twenty years:

26th and Market, The American Journal of Poetry, After Shocks Anthology, And Know This Place Anthology, Avatar, Amarillo Bay Review, The Bitter Southerner, Blast Furnace Magazine, Blesok (Shine), Breakwater, CafÈ Review, Cedar Hill Review, Chamber Four, Cincinnati Review, Comstock Review, Connecticut Review, DuPage Valley Review, Elixir Magazine, Hartskill Review, Hamilton-Stone Review, Jefferson Review, Nassau Review, North American Review, Open 24 Hours, Pagetica, Partyzan, Poetry Southeast, ReVerb Magazine, Roque Dalton Anthology, Southern Indiana Review, Spectrum Magazine, Unbound Press, Under the Sun, Vietnam War Poetry Anthology. Vilenica International Literary Anthology.

I owe thanks as well to almost every person I've ever met for teaching me something about life, but especially to a few who helped me explore the art and craft of writing:

Ralph Angel, David Bartholomy, Stephen Dobyns, Matthew Graham, Rick Jackson, Ron Mitchell, Victoria Redel, Betsy Scholl, Natasha Saje, Leslie Ullman, Michael Waters, Tom Wilhelmus, David Wojahn, and especially to my teacher and friend, Jack Myers, who always told me, "You can break any rule you want, as long as you know the rule and why you're breaking it."

CONTENTS

I.

- 21 Black Ice
- 22 In Memoriam: Hunter S. Thompson
- 23 Mama Said There'd Be Days Like This
- 24 Garage Sale
- 25 Montreal Winter
- 26 Baling Hay
- 27 Associations
- 29 Forty Years Ago
- 30 Running the Voodoo Down
- 35 Traveling
- 37 Clotheslines
- 38 Where Were You When I Needed You, Jack Kerouac
- 40 Bridge
- 41 Driving by My Childhood Home Forty Years Later
- 42 The Truth About Mangoes
- 44 Memorial Weekend, 2017
- 45 Antique Show in New Harmony, Indiana
- 46 Generation Gap
- 48 On the 50th Anniversary of Murder in Money, Mississippi, Dark Energy Is Discovered in Space
- 49 Why Uncle Vern Quit Driving
- 50 Cycles
- 51 Lunch Time at the Blue River Inn
- 52 Hearing the First Music
- 53 The Man in the Moon
- 54 Broken
- 56 Almost Music
- 57 The Immigrants—1929
- 58 Popcorn Sutton
- 59 Cody's Diner
- 60 Dancer
- 62 Note to Jill:
- 64 When the Stars Go Dark

II.

- 69 Meditations of the Jungle Ambush
- 70 The VFW Rededicates the War Monument On the Courthouse Lawn on Memorial Day

71 When a Zero Means Everything
72 Absence
74 Thirty Years from the TET Offensive
75 Translation
76 On Le La Street in Hue, 1968 & 2005
77 The Holy Citadel in Hue, 1968 and 2008
78 In Country, 1967
79 The Memorial Wall
82 Becoming the Dark
84 The Art of Deep Breathing
85 March Is the Cruelest Month
87 The Warrior's Elegy
90 Eating with Chopsticks in Vietnam
91 At The Museum of Modern Art in New York City I Wondered:
92 On the Streets of Saigon in the 21st Century
93 Operation Lancaster, 1967
96 On Veteran's Day a Vietnam Veteran Reads the Names of American Soldiers Killed in the Iraqi War
97 Peace

III.
101 Dinner at Lorenzo's
102 My Shame in 1958
103 Art of the Deal
105 South of Atlanta on I-75, I Find America
107 There's a Lesson for Us on the Perfume River
108 Posse Commitatis at Stating Rock—Winter 2016
109 An Ordinary Man Goes Shopping at Kroger's
111 Elegy for Charles Darwin
112 Suicide in High School
113 Plumber's Hymn # 1
114 Collateral Damage
115 Anniversary
116 The Pursuit of Knowledge
118 Blurbing
119 Eli's Elegy
121 Oakland Park Cemetery, Atlanta, On a Sunday Morning in June
122 Between Nogales and the Border
123 At a Small Mexican Diner
124 My Childhood Is Dead—Long Live My Childhood
126 Sunday Morning Synchronicity

127 Breakfast at Denny's
129 The English Professor Reflects on Career Choices
130 Elegy for a Postal Worker
132 Free Market Enterprise

IV.
135 A Balancing Act
136 How to Find the Animal Inside
137 Some Thoughts on Humility
141 Tabla Rosa
143 A Fisherman's Grace
144 Hop Along
146 On Giving My Bicycle Away to Charity
147 The Garvin Gate Blues Festival in Louisville, Kentucky
149 Polemics
150 August Blues on the River
151 A Change of Scenery
152 Climbing in the Garden of the Gods at Harrisburg, Illinois
153 Interstate 24
154 Addition
155 New Orleans Fais Do Do
156 Honestly
157 Peeling Potatoes
159 How We Were What We Never Became
160 Naturally Unnatural
161 Sonnet of True Love
162 Poem About Writing a Novel
163 The Continuous Positive Airway Pressure Machine
164 Smoker's Wake
165 National Anthem
166 Out of Focus
167 The Changing Rain
168 Vision Problems
170 The Garden
171 Tune-Up
172 Measuring
177 Alter Idem
179 Snapshots
185 Dia de los Muertos

Prologue

The Brief History of Poetry

So, for me this poem thing kicked off
with Enheduanna, high priestess of Ur
who, four thousand years before
Shakespeare fancied his first sonnet,
laid language in the open arms of love,
caressed it till Sappho sexed up Homer's
wine dark sea that the waves might bear
Shelley, Keats and Blake to shore where
rhyme languished till Eliot and Pound
blew smoke up its ass and triggered
an addiction to substance over form.
Now, coughing phlegm and lighting Kools,
subject to seizures and bad breath, my words
drink bourbon unrestrained in some seedy
backwater Bukowski kind of bar awaiting
new Strophes that may never show
or, even if they do, buy another round.

I.

So we beat on, boats against the current, borne back ceaselessly into the past.
—F. Scott Fitzgerald

Black Ice

Those stories of an entire life
flashing by in seconds—lies—the stories
are lies. What you remember when the ice
on the black asphalt of Route 87 levitates
your car, offers it to the dead stars, and hangs you
confused between air and wild rock face
in Upstate New York, what you remember

is the train station in Cuernavaca. You're standing
next to Roceria. Diesel fuel, roses, sweat,
and vanilla tangle in your nose as her black jungle
of hair brushes goodbye across your face. What you
think about as the car bounces off the guardrail
marching backward down the cliff to the cadence
of metal shredding, what you think about

is your last breakfast in Mexico. Her tiny wrist
sprinkles chili powder over grapefruit
as the sunrise falls in red grains through the green trees.
You've never seen anyone do that before and you wonder
how the memory of this spice can ripen
the memory of her sweetness so much
that six thousand miles and thirty years later,
when the car finally stops spinning,
all you taste as you bite through your lip
is the warm, metallic flow of regret.

In Memoriam: Hunter S. Thompson

Time held me green and dying though I sang in chains like the sea.
—Dylan Thomas

After all, it was HST not JFK, so I graded freshman essays
the day he put a bullet through his cruel, drug-crazed gonzo genius,

and sipped bourbon from a square glass while birds and barren trees
mocked the passing of a generation that wanted to get life right

but never did, that fought a war then fought a war to end the war,
that blessed and cursed itself as caretaker of its own mortality.

I imagined Hunter alone, the wind lifting the skirt of his mind
to expose his hope, numbed and withered by the constant wash

of chemicals through his addled brain, his hope that if misery fuels
self-destruction, then so must love. You know, the kind of love

forcing children to stick their hands in beehives and grope for honey,
driving a man to wander river banks late at night, counting stars, listening

as waves from coal barges break over frozen stones on the cut bank
to the warm rhythm of a woman's heartbeat, the kind of love

that brings a boy to the front of rolling tanks in Tiananmen Square,
a girl to give up her child, a soldier to fall on a grenade, the feeling

hidden in us all that something exists somewhere more worthy
than the self. This is what finally killed Hunter Thompson, not bullets,

not drugs, not even the indifference of new generations —the same
cross that Jesus chose to hang on, the same need to fuel the myth

of love that grants us grace beyond humanity, if only in shadows,
like the moonflower opens its petals and bears its soul to the darkness.

Mama Said There'd be Days like This

Van Morrison croons softly
as I peel potatoes and stare out
the kitchen window this evening

until memories pop into my head,
those ones that hold me close
to sanity in a world gone mad

of days when time was not the enemy,
when I lit a joint & sat back staring
into a high blue sky, when mortality

did not leak like dirty motor oil
over my adolescent lust for every
girl on every day of high school

and those nights when laughter
quenched my misery from broken love
that rose like bile in my throat, or different

seasons when leaves changed colors
and the colors brought a first snow, when
dew and the wonder of a pine tree's scent

mingled with stars, a time when time
did not exist, only red and blue dreams
floating like flowers on an infinite river of life.

Garage Sale

In my parents' attic clutter metastasizes.
Cardboard urns
labeled "mixed shit" spin

in deadly patterns, stack and rise,
crimp and crumble, bend
and split beyond control.
These contain the cells of life
once lived—here, a broken ashtray,
there a worn ball glove, in a corner
report cards and a dusty shoebox
filled with faded snapshots
of some childhood Christmas
neither my sister nor I can remember.
What use is this folded flag,
symbol for an armistice
no family reaches until death?
What we wish to be true rarely is
anywhere except in memories.

Mothballs swaddle the scent
of my mother's high school sweater
in a musty shroud of newspaper
and wool blankets.

Above the coos of doves
that nest in arches and patter of rats
over rafter beams, I dream the scratch
of needle on vinyl from the ancient
phonograph 78s. A Ray Charles piano
sears the air with dark blues,
my father's favorite sound.
Two silhouettes dance, dusty
in the yellow memory of dusk
that has slipped in through the sill
of a single window, never opened,
never used.

Montreal Winter

for Wendy

Language is what I sleep with
since you left, letters tying down
ropes of thought that moan
like mooring cables stretched
along this ice-scarred lake front.
Words walk with me between the cars
and snowflakes into O'Grady's Pub.
We rent a pool table, wrap
our fingers around a crooked cue
and play your favorite game.
But, I don't feel the tingle
of their anticipation
along my radial nerve
as the cue ball spins.
Verbs don't dance the way you do
to Carly Simon's song on the jukebox,
or drink O'Grady's white wine,
so cheap it doubles for varnish remover.
Nouns don't laugh
or cry as the numbered balls
all roll in different directions
and clear the green cloth that feels
as smooth as the inside of your left thigh
against the palm of my hand.

Baling Hay

The Wabash shrinks and swells each spring.
Somewhere above flood stage, its peristaltic rage
scoops topsoil from low-lying farmland,

the current churning it into a black lava
of trees limbs and trash that may or may not
grow into hay when summer ends

if the flood fades below the river's banks
in time to seed the fields. Nature reminds us
we decide what we want, not what we will have.

One fall fifty years ago I baled hay on J.P.'s farm.
The rough timothy chaffed my forearms and the salt
from my sweat stung like a thousand tiny bees.

My brother stopped the tractor long enough to offer
a sip of tepid water from a bright orange jug.
He had knocked up J.P.'s daughter and I was helping

pay off his shame. The crickets sang and ragweed
filled my lungs. From the forest beyond the field
a hint of honeysuckle rose and misted over us.

I was a man for that moment. The habit of pretending
to believe became the habit of believing.
I tossed bales from wagon to conveyor belt

and stacked them neatly in the loft, enough to feed
the stock all winter. While my brother parked
the tractor I walked to the river,

the same one that spilled over the field
two months before. The sun poured its light
across the water as all my future ghosts emerged

as shadows near the bank, and drank like deer in the dusk.

Associations

Beneath the bushes that circle
the Christian Science Reading Room
a woman's compact, mirror broken,
lies open and empty
like a shucked clamshell.
I'm walking my dog and thinking
how one thing leads to another, how
Mary Baker Eddy parlayed
her fear of doctors into a world religion,
how the dog pisses where other dogs do.
Everything feels linked this morning,
 a cosmology that explains
why a useless make-up kit litters
the doorway to a library full
of ineffective information and both
remind me of the best time in my life,
serious laughter and comedic hopes,
all too real when applied to a generation
bent on self-destruction. Oh, you know
exactly what I mean, that era when Quixote
sold Mambrino's helmet for bell bottom jeans
and a nickel bag, when his Sancho Panza
wore no bra under her tie-dyed tee shirt
and draft cards were for lighting Lucky Strikes.
Just last night, my two friends David
and David were trying to convince me
over bottles of red wine that the Sixties
were more than my romantic memory,
more than fashion and pharmaceuticals,
guitar prophets and sex in elevators, but less
than a revolution or the resurrection
of humanity. Today, I'm sober, skeptical
of our recall and all our viewpoints,
wondering if that last best chance
for Utopia was the same dream-colored
make-up it's always been, housed

between the chromed shutters of each era's wars
and applied in the broken mirror of history
until it's exhausted, empty, and cast away.

Forty Years Ago

I fished a farm pond
full of perch with a woman.
Surrounded by shrubs and oak trees,

guarded by cattails and nettles,
encircled by a field of winter wheat,
we cast lures into the wet, languid darkness.

No one can define that kind of love anymore,
at least in a world made without it.
We were hooked, landed, and couldn't breathe.

Running the Voodoo Down

My clock radio blasts
me into dawn.
I see the flick of a wrist
outside my window
and the morning news lands
between the sidewalk and a step.
The boy rides on
singing no song loudly
as I retrieve the paper, an unshaven dog
in slippers and oversized robe.
Sandy the nurse jogs by, waves
disapprovingly at my first cigarette.
The only conscious drunk in town
bends, scoops cans from the curb
across the street and places them
into a plastic bag, hoping
to recycle them into bottles
of Wild Irish Rose by sunset.
Southern Railway cattle cars
whistle through the crossing
like empty martini glasses clacking
and I am alone in the middle of nothing,
the center of everything.

I open the newspaper.
Swarms of small words buzz
into the gray light like bees
escaping the hive.
I let them go to watch Mrs. Martin
slowly drive toward the drugstore.
Her left front tire, out of balance
since Mr. Martin died of cancer,
flaps on wet asphalt: thump-hiss
What if...What if...What if...

What if
the spent bullet that struck my chest
beneath an open flack jacket
thirty years ago isn't spent,
is killing me slowly?
What if it had been fired from point blank range,
a bolt from a god in black pajamas?
What if what I had slapped and caught with an open hand
was the hole it left, if my blood had congealed to paste,
and my lungs lost their vacuum?
What if the last things I saw were lines
on my best friend's right palm closing my eyes?

A horn blows.
My neighbor ushers his sullen child
up the steps of a yellow school bus.
"Morning Jim. What's doing?"
"Reading the paper."
But what I'm doing is
glancing at pink flowers on white cotton underwear
pressed against the storm door across the street
as Marcy lets her bulldog out to pee.
My eyes fold an oak tree into the cloudless sky.
I frisk my pockets for egg money,
listen to a hum inside the daylight lifting fog.
It sounds like stardust weeping.
Darkness ends around me the way my father
would have ended it, with a pledge
that all things dim grow progressively brighter.
He always saw the new day
as something more than it really was.
Yesterday the coroner, who reeked
of talcum powder and isopropyl,
lifted retinas, one good iris, even aqueous humor
from my father's face. Someone else will get his eyes
but he willed his sight to me.

I change my clothes
and on my morning walk, pass a vacant house

on Hart Street remembering
this same doorway Christmas morning, 1955.
Our gold Plymouth stops
curbside and Dad leaves a turkey
and three small toys on the porch.
I watch his lips move—all you get from life
is what you give to others—but the sound
of his voice is swallowed by my sobs.
I thought the toys were mine.
Out of breath
I stop at unconscious attention
on a square of dying grass at the courthouse lawn.
A sculptured eagle on a stone spike carries names
skyward... Isiah Beadles, Isaac Decker, Josiah Palmer...
the weathered letters shine, faint window lights
far across a cold lake.
The 58th Indiana Volunteers built this marker
in 1865, a cenotaph for the living.
Is memory prophecy? These letters, scrambled,
reappeared a hundred years later, on dog tags
10,000 miles away smelling
of cordite and gunpowder. The groans
erupting from the black ground, the hunger
for silence—all the same.
Once, before a ballgame, I found four combat medals
buried beneath argyle socks in an old trunk.
I remember Dad snatching them from my hand
as if they were burning matches.
"The sins of the fathers...", he whispered.
The same ceramic guilt that glazed his proud eyes
coated them again when I was carried home a hero
and broken from Vietnam, like a cheap watch
that keeps losing time.

I cross the street and enter
Cody's Diner. Eggs fry, bacon splatters,
warm coffee seeps from a worn auto-drip.
Racing forms crackle in calloused hands.
The smoke from seven cigarettes crawls upward

like cobwebs on the grease stained wall.
The corner stool is covered with a funeral
wreath of freshly cut flowers.
No one tries to make "sorry your dad died"
sound sincere with breakfast.

Back home after breakfast an angel falls.
I catch him by his wings, and when I open my hand,
a moth escapes.
Blue-haired women
carry crock pots stuffed with ham and pie tins
crusted with cooked apples to my front door.
Like my father, their vision of life seems nourished
by their attention to death.
The street sings a dirge that only I hear
in the wail of a small terrier tied to a fence post.

My father once drank a fifth of Beefeater's gin,
drove to the city pound and, crying, clipped
the chain off the gate.
While he locked himself
inside the bottle, forty dogs ran free.

By noon, I begin searching
the same bottle for the key
he dropped in there.
The bottle empties at dusk. I disappear
by becoming part
of the neighborhood around me.

Gray men drive home from work,
schoolgirls hopscotch,
skipping over scarred concrete.
None of them know how close to death
 this day brought them. What would they
change and why would they change it,
even if they did?

The neighbor's son leans into their magnolia bush,
kissing white blossoms, but I'm the one caressed
by the boughs, carried by fragrance into a softer world,
where Holloway suckers last all day,
where bicycle lock chains lie unused in an open garage,
where deadbolts exist in science fiction books
and the smell of leather ball gloves and Neat's foot oil
mixes easily with the taste of my gin…

I begin to see in this boy's blameless smile
the reason to go on my father saw in mine.

A phone rings.
Someone calls a dog home.
A cat in heat squeals.
I fall asleep for the first time
with no link to my own beginning,
with no fear of my own end.

Awakened at midnight
on the same front porch where I began,
I hear the hum of cicadas
as the flow of waterfalls.
Starlings and sparrows sing with larger voices
songs of a smaller realm.
On the arm of the porch swing a pregnant mantis
steps cautiously toward space. She can't fly
and has eaten the father of her children.
Overhead the sky is so clear
I can see through the stars, each one
a window into some long-hidden attic,
holding my father's ashes and his light.
An attic much like the one across the street
where a new father nails sheetrock
beneath a bare light bulb, each hammer blow
a shout against the darkness, each panel hung
a larger world for his newly born child.

Traveling

Driving through Mississippi
in the 21st Century, there's nothing new
in my vision except a sign flashing through
the back-lit fog, a silent glossolalia of light that chases
small birds and sinners from the dangers of the neon night:
    "Jesus Is Waiting"

and so am I, for one small worm hole in this wall of gray air,
another galaxy for my restless mind, another woman
to replace the one I lost this morning in a hail
of frozen words and slammed doors. It's never easy
being a prick, but I've always been successful.

Too bad Jesus can't follow me
from His motel room of martyrdom, help me
find the inside of my heart where love wants to be
available always and by the hour. It's somewhere
in Biloxi this time, where the Dairy Queen sells beer
and fish factories ruin the bay with shrimp offal. We could
panhandle along the beach and brawl our way through
nightclubs stuffed like sardine tins with servicemen.
What a sight—Jesus and me puking fried clams,
dry heaving like beached flounders, or pissing
up some brick wall behind the Waffle House.

Too bad... I see Him hanging in my rearview mirror
with a supernatural flame on a billboard of fluorescent
alphabet disappearing around the next curve, replaced
by the faint outline of barbeque joints, tar paper
shacks, swamps, and rusted out trucks jacked up
on cinder blocks. I'm somewhere between Biloxi
and Hell in Rural Americana on a funky stretch
of highway that seems more memory than prophecy,
more a deja vu I've traveled through on the way
to someplace else again. Maybe Jesus knows why
the night is all that ever travels with me, how I picked

Biloxi when the land runs into ocean on a dozen
better beaches along the Gulf Coast, or why motion
keeps me still. If he does, he's not talking. All I hear
above the whine of warm night wind are clouds
as they scrape their tongues against the teeth of the moon.

Clotheslines

I don't see them much these days, not since Laundromats
& Sears credit cards & Master Charge & affordable Maytags.
America,
land of microchips
    fiber optics
    titanium alloys
    HD Tv
    & space age plastic,

                has ceased to hang its laundry
like my mother did once
on taut lines of hemp between the sag of an old chicken coup,
the glint of a gold Plymouth & the taste of those Eisenhower
decade dreams—2.5 perfect children & a quiet menopause.

I'm told that's a good thing, like a pay raise at Christmas,
or one of dad's sure winners at the track But, I miss
the childhood smell of bleached light and soap woven
into fresh cut grass & rinsed through the fabric
of an early May day.

My mother never seemed to tire
of reaching in her apron for those old wooden clothespins,
or chasing the sleeve of my father's white shirt
as it fluttered along the line in a fit.

Her fatigue came later as I grew older, her dreams
vaguer with the miles between us, & whatever it was
that she had hoped for through me got frayed
around the edges of my acid trips, bad
marriages, lost jobs, & soiled visions, fading

with the wash of years over her face.

Where Were You When I Needed You, Jack Kerouac

Above me stars tremble
like quartz flakes in a candle-lit cave.
My mind is silent
as it dreams, until
I swallow four tabs of No-Doz
with mescaline, then it screams
in colors while the Oldsmobile
sheds highway
like a blue snake escapes
old skin and begins again.
Turning right, turning left, turning
right into a labyrinth of tequila
and adobe homes, I'm switch backed
by Pemex stations, cantinas, and mountains
that rise beside me in the salmon colored
smog of dawn. The more I learn
of language, the less I know of life
and loss. The asphalt melts
into a pearl beach, a ribbon of jet set
stores, juke joints, a KFC, and forlorn
taco stands. Acapulco, Mexico sings
a brown Coltrane song of concrete and sand,
discordance with purpose, clarity
in confusion. Cruise ship klaxons and car
horns blow the Deguelo of an all-night
mariachi band and produce markets of tanned
flesh call me toward Roceria.
Her tongue pours over my mind
like warm Kama Sutra oil and the quickening
of sunlight traps me in my own shadow.

"That old black magic has me in its spell
That old black magic that you weave so well"

J'ai L'ai rackets and bullfight posters,
Federales so young they still laugh,

grapefruits, bananas, mangoes, and grapes,
the smell of chili powder tied
in humid chords of air with café con leche
and cow dung, everything is real
including the nothing that hangs
on the tourist board outside Sandborn's diner
where I park the car.
I've driven all these miles and years for a note
from her and found this posted on the sterile cork:
Michael call home.
Single White Female needs ride to Baja—will party.
Lost wallet found—empty.
For sale, moped—slightly bent frame.

"I can't dance don't ask me."

What makes a single kiss
final one day and the next day leaves you feeling
as if the stove's left on and the whole meal's burning?

Roceria once told me that only Jack
Kerouac knew the secret of life and I said,
"What? Gallo Port wine in a glass of despair?"
She said, "All humans are really sharks," and climbed
aboard a crowded bus with her back to me,
her hair braided and swaying, a black metronome
of promise that has clicked through these past
years of memory and brought me back
to the Mexican beach where we met.
She must have four kids now
and a frequent black eye from her husband
as a badge of love. I must be crazy, still searching
for a goddess who was never more than human
and alone on a school holiday. I must be
that shark of Jack's, eating everything around me
and swimming constantly, just to stay alive.

Bridge

On the deck of the Delta Queen, I'm eating
fried clams and watching as working men haul cables
across the Ohio for the new suspension bridge.

Some braid heavy wire, some row skiffs.
Broadsided by the current, their flannel shirts
bob and spin like leaves in an autumn breeze,

their sweat reminiscent of the days when this river
meant more than something to get across on the way
to an office full of data or suburb full of dreams,

when flat boats hauled farm produce and corn liquor,
and the deckhands, fresh immigrants from every corner
of the European continent, fought off river pirates—

cruel men to whom death was just business—
for a piece of life that would always lie beyond
their desperate grasp, a dream that kept them moving,

to spill into something larger not knowing as they went
that no matter what obstacles they crossed,
the flow toward it would never stop even as the sea arrived.

Driving by My Childhood Home Forty Years Later

The paint peels and the magnolia tree,
sawn to stump, is pedestal for a birdbath,
foundation for a trellis of honeysuckle vines.

From the door on the west corner, my room opened
outward once till nailed shut, a father's failed effort
to keep his young son from self-destructive wanderlust.

The pear tree withers, the neighbors have died,
and I'd like to look inside, view the rooms
where grandma came to live and nanny us

when mom joined the workforce so we could buy
our first color TV. Grandma used to prop sis and me
on her goose down mattress, warm beneath the quilts,

while she knitted sweaters slowly and tried to ignore
the chill that came from knowing even time has its limits.
On Saturdays, we'd watch Buffalo Bob Barker

pull Howdy Doody's puppet strings on Channel Six,
thankful school was out and waiting while the neighborhood
came alive with Schwinn bikes, hula hoops,

and the weekly wiffle ball game. Not one of us ever
knew a drive-by shooting or the collapse of world finance.
The fear of being trapped by boredom drove us crazy.

It festered in our guts till
this curdled milk of small town ennui—the idea
that happiness is always somewhere else—steered us

separate ways to larger cities and more exotic dreams,
to seek the lives we left before our deaths arrived.

The Truth About Mangoes

My mother called bell peppers
"mangoes" and would not stand for my correction.

The damn—a word she rarely used
for fear of sounding coarse—things were green.

She forgot they were red and yellow also,
and the fact that one grew in groves by the sea

while the other grew hollow with a lust for chili.
Nothing mattered except what her mind saw

when she heard the word "mangoes." To think
of her this way requires a constant longing.

She was the horizon,
a vanishing point, near but never reachable,

a shadow full of substance,
a ghost with flowing blood and warm tears

at the times she crushed an aspirin between two spoons
and fed it to my childish fever with a drop of honey,

or taught me how to foxtrot without tripping
before my high school prom. Hell, she even

fed my dad with silence, not speaking
for weeks when he spent a single night drunk.

A quiet life was what she valued and so returned
it to us with what she knew of love. For her fear

of feeling joy, her wish to neither brag nor complain
but bear life in silence as every godly wife was taught

in Eisenhower days, god killed her with Lou Gehrig's curse, though watching baseball was her only vice.

Memorial Weekend, 2017

R.I.P. Gregg Allman

Take any street in any town in the USA
& place, an orange cat, deceased by auto,
on the warm asphalt. Its tongue lolls
to the left side and both eyes stare upward
as if awaiting the next roiling lump of clouds
from which to sculpt a dream of mice.
Not an unusual sight in a world of hurried
& indifferent drivers who will slaughter
whatever pauses in their path to the nearest
barbeque or parade—it's the American way
to commemorate the dead we do not know
with hot dogs and marching bands.

But on this day a small group of wild turkeys
has left the copse beside the road and circled
the cat's corpse in a solemn wake.

I see this strange scene only because some
fool wasting time has turned his cell phone on
and captured it in a video, and I, another fool
wasting time, now watch it on the internet.

The birds step & cluck in perfect rhythm
with the clank & clatter of distant horns
& drums from a parade in the town square,
a dance of grief they share though unaware,
a prayer to some god they cannot worship,
a flight of fancy taken by birds that do not fly,
a song they hear the cat sing, but dare not repeat,
an end to music as the music goes on.

Antique Show in New Harmony, Indiana

Everything gets old,
but some things
gain value as they rust and crack,
peel and fade into the past
like the Rolling Stones
or a buffalo head nickel.
A white-haired farmer
says to the woman next to me,
"Damn teapot cost more
than my old Ford truck did
when I bought it new
and the spout's already cracked."

My first real bicycle had whitewall tires,
a red frame, white streamers,
wire basket, and no training wheels.
Dad brought it home one summer
as if he finally knew I had grown
from him, and yet was no longer him.
It was our first step away from each other
and cost a day's pay.
I'd give twice that
to find one here today, leaning
against the end of this table
by the Mason jars and a broken cuckoo clock.

It's odd how the present can trap us
in the past. Lately, all my dreams happen
at 2:00AM, the hour he died. I wake
on the edge of my own mortality
with an image of some old argument
proving nothing more than we grew into
similar men who might have been friends
if born in the same era, if wounded
in the same wars. Instead, the world made us
enemies that came with passing years
to love each other once again.

Generation Gap

When the moon is full my son transforms
himself. He and his friends leave
white suburbia behind by simply driving
their Levis four inches down below the waist,
steering stocking caps over straight hair,
and playing rap songs through devices they mistakenly
call "sub-wolfers." Our neighbors, unaccustomed
to loud thumps accompanied by strings
of words that rhyme with bitch, cock, gat, and clit,
have called the cops four times.
"What makes you want to be someone you're not?"
I asked my son right before
shutting the circuit breaker to his room down
and chasing his friends out.
His lips made sounds like bees buzzing—ism
ism   ism   ism—Schism my gism.
But, appropriated cultural noise answers no question
I couldn't answer for myself on a spring night in '66.
After I throttled one recalcitrant burst of acne
into submission and wiped it away with Stridex,
after my parents handed me a set of vinyl luggage
and a bus ticket to some faraway private college
and after Mona refused to jack me off in the driver's seat
of my '57 Belair because she was left-handed, I walked
into darkness with that question, like plasma, pulsing
through my mind. Before the night ended my friends
and I stole a case of beer from a neighbor's
back porch and drank till the stars exploded in bursts
of pepperoni pizza over Converse high tops.
We screamed "get fucked" at a State Trooper
as we sailed past the old refinery on Highway 41
in a '63 Dodge Charger borrowed from my father,
top-ended and almost sobered by the wind at 110 mph.
We swam the White River naked, each one daring
the others to go first. And I did, as if the habit of being led
had suddenly become my own desire and the distance

between this shore and that one might be measured
in breast strokes and ragged breath alone, without regard
for current, snags, or a tricky undertow. I wanted
to be someone else if only for a moment, to scream at the world
"You don't scare me" and show my friends
that slight tilt of the head, the arrogance
of young manhood that threatened to drown us all.

On the 50th Anniversary of Murder in Money, Mississippi, Dark Energy Is Discovered in Space

Today, astronomers caught the universe expanding,
the density of dusk dancing with rhythmic energy,
whole galaxies split apart like diamonds. "No one knew

till now that the dark outside created light within,"
they said, as if this "dark energy" were a formless god
beyond our control, devoid of our influence, on fire.

Emmett Till learned the opposite fact fifty years ago
when he arrived in Money on the bus from Chicago
without the knowledge that traveling south would alter him,

make him into something less than human, without the cowed
deference that enslaved yet might have saved him. Two white men,
whose dark energy was born and growing inside light skin,

dragged Emmett to a river bank and beat blue his blackness.
Then, as if one death was not enough, they put a bullet
into his head and, with no remorse, went home to dinner.

Why Uncle Vern Quit Driving

Once a year my uncle rose at 3AM,
opened his first Stag Beer, and stuffed
a turkey for Thanksgiving dinner.
At noon my aunt drove him slowly
to our home where the family gathered
and it was custom for Dad to state,
"the bird is baked and so is Uncle Vern."
We'd all laugh and time passed
more blessing than curse. I'd pretend the fun
wouldn't fade. I held on to that trick of youth
as long as possible, even drove ten miles
across state lines years later to buy Stag beer
until it was laid to rest by corporate merger
just after Uncle Vern by cancer.
That's about when the taste went out
of a lot of things for me.
I'm sure it had to do with what I learned
at his wake, one of those mysteries unveiled
that destroys a perfect memory.
Some distant cousin told the story of Vern's
first wife, the one before my aunt that I knew
nothing about, how he drove drunk
into another car, killed her and his daughter,
and never drove again. I tried empathy,
even infused images of my recent time in war
—the blasts of mortars, the bursts of bodies,
the lessening of all life to primal urge—
on twisted metal and burned rubber.
But it did not work.
His reluctance to drive seemed
a frail repentance to me, a small gesture
for a heinous crime that lost him my respect.
I did not know then
it was the best he could do.
I did not know then
even a feather will bruise if dropped
from the proper height.

Cycles

It is a perfect day in the park as ten young men swirl
across the concrete court. Their foreheads bead with sweat,
breath leaking like steam from hot engines straining

to pull the weight of immortality up the long grade
of adolescence. My dogs tug their leashes, the crunching
paws scatter frost like dust over the last patches of summer grass.

They want that basketball the boys bounce with the same pure pain
that constricts my chest each time I see a hawk ride an air current,
a foal chase its mother's shadow across a timothy field, or children

smile at dawn and collapse the whole world upon itself.
Beside the park entrance, a small lake reflects a woman
dangling like a crazed and crippled puppet as she does

T'ai Chi and, without speaking, turns her flesh into the language
of air. I listen for meaning as the wind breaks the morning mist
over her outstretched arms and slows her down.

I am a boy again who lands the huge bass lurking
near the shore. I see the perfect rainbow sunlight scales
from silver fins when the fish rises, feel sweat leaking

in my palms as I crank the reel, hear crickets and frogs, how
the breeze lifts the limbs of willows and spreads their leaves
just as the line snaps and the fish flops back into the water

where it must still wait in the wet shadows for my return.

Lunch Time at the Blue River Inn

A Wandering Jew steers through
the wilderness of duct work,
bearing green leaves on a lush journey
over avant-garde art and Betty Davis posters
as the goat of Azaziel once carried sins
into the ancient night
without knowledge, without desire.
The cook stirs wild rice soup
while a young farmer sits on a stool
and reads a prophecy of calloused
monotony in his own palms.
Porcelain cups string along a counter top,
unstrung pearls, as Jean, the waitress,
pours coffee into them with trembling hands.
"Twenty years ago, I was going to be a dancer,"
she says. Her left eye twitches and she folds
forks and spoons into paper napkins. Soon,
Jean's dreams echo around the noon crowd,
like rain that splatters overhead on the tin roof,
rolls off, and disappears in an arid, yearning earth.

Hearing the First Music

for Jimmy Hayes

The cut bank on the Connecticut River
framed itself with graduated rocks
long before the first man played music,
I listened to the xylophonic current on the stones
and stared eye to eye with a brown hawk
between a floor of treetops and rafters made from clouds.

Then I scaled the long trail strung with blue spruce
and mountain vetch, each step
toward the crest lifting me through light,
pulling cross-hatched shadows through my chest,
and the song the wind sang in the green ferns
sounded like butterflies falling.

Above empty tobacco barns, deserted cattle farms,
and horse paths littered with shopping malls, I stepped
over pterosaurs etched in shale by the same water
that snapped their wings and swept their souls
into the river bed a million years before,
their shrieks echoing along with the rocky scree.

Sitting on a rock to rest,
my ragged breath escaped from life below
and mingled with the mountain mist.
The weight of blood and bone seem to rise
like a blue kite my father flew for me when I was ten.
I became a raindrop that would not fall again, even in the rain.

The Man in the Moon

This morning as I drank my coffee, Henry Tauzin stood
swaying like saw grass in the jungle of my mind. The ebb

and flow of his body spilled over a pale notion till he became
my man in the moon, a myth reflected beneath banyans

as those trees dipped and swirled with the monsoon breeze.
The bamboo played a tango so hypnotic and hollow

I hardly noticed another whistle, the metallic trill
of an RPG ripping through the melody like off key fusion jazz.

Henry heard it coming though. He opened his arms wide,
embraced the blast to keep shrapnel from shattering my skull.

I caught his left arm in my lap—a beautiful tan Creole arm
ridged with sculpted muscle smoking like a sandalwood joss stick—

gathered the rest of him up and placed him in a body bag
as the moon surrendered all its promise to the numb shadows of dawn.

Broken

His ghost must still be there
on the barstool even though the bar
is gone, destroyed by fire decades ago.
I see him clearly in my mind
puffing Winchester filtered cigars
instead of unfiltered Lucky Strikes,
aware of but uncaring for the irony
contained in his emphysema as he exhaled
wheezing like a spent squeeze box
in perfect harmony to a weird polka
playing on the Wurlitzer.

He wanted my body.
His was used up and twenty head
of horses were corralled nearby, sold
but unready for saddle. Someone dumb
had to climb on, hang on, ride on, fall off,
and get back on until the nags could be
trained for tourists who paid to play
pretend cowboys every weekend
in the mild Catskill summer. It was '69.
Broken by war, I lived on cheap beer
and bad dreams, afraid that some sins
could never be confessed and penance
worked only through self-ruin.

It was love at first sight, he for my youth
and I for the chance to pound away my past
at ten dollars a horse. I bruised the earth
with my bucked off backside for a month.
Those horses saved my life with pain.
The sound of his gruff laughter
echoed like a fog horn in a hurricane,
a ricochet off a tin wall, or an eagle's wing
in a rain storm if I were given to hyperbole.
Instead, I'll just repeat the elegance

of his advice as he screamed at each failure
"Get up. You ain't broken, yore jest bent."

Almost Music

My father bought a player piano.
He and his friend Bob stopped
for a beer in a backwoods bar near
Mt. Carmel, Illinois. The owner refused
to serve them at first because Bob was black
even though we lived close by and LBJ
signed the Civil Rights Act a year before.
In the corner near the jukebox, this old piano
stood, a remnant of another era
covered with dust, out-of-date magazines,
scars and scratches from barroom brawls,
& a single water ring from someone's
empty glass. It played "Roll out the Barrel"
if you dropped a nickel in the slot, but two keys
were stuck & you had to not mind
the out-of-place caesura they caused.
On the spot, Dad offered to buy
the damn thing as long as he and Bob
could drink a Falls City beer & listen to that
song before they hoisted it on the pickup truck
& brought it home where it played crippled versions
in our basement till they both died many decades later.
The piano plays the same song still, but the spool
has warped and the notes seem more out of tune
each time we try & sing along.

The Immigrants—1929

Grandpa healed great locomotives, herding them
out of Southern Railway shops along the veins of tracks
connecting both coasts to the Hoosier heartland. Paid enough
for bread and a few of those potatoes the Irish learned to love,
he brought home a bag of coal every week in winter
to fire the iron stove rising from the floor like a black orchid.
That stove split the house into kitchen and parlor.
Grandma bought "blue john" milk from a horse drawn wagon
and enough sugar to make the oatmeal taste better than paste,
but all that luxury ended when the stock market crashed.
The Southern trains quit running. Not afraid of hard labor
Grandpa took odd jobs at first, then hired on the WPA
to clear brush, swing a pick, bust rock into gravel and build
a hundred farm roads that still crisscross Gibson county.
Depression had more to do with cash than self-esteem.
If he plowed no garden no garden got plowed, fed no chickens
no chickens were fed, and dinner wasn't as long on presentation
as it was practicality in those lean days, those days they learned
that living with need was better than giving in or up.
Grandma shared no patience with wastrels in her house.
My dad and uncle "Ding" split wood or went to bed hungry,
although a hobo might sample apple pie if the budget
had allowed for a show of wealth on a particular week.
Rules sustained their home:
Treat others better than you would treat yourself.
If you must steal to keep from going hungry, go hungry.
Curse only when the Cardinals lose the pennant.
Never take a drink on Sunday or use spittoons in the house.
Say nothing at the dinner table that doesn't sound grateful.
Show all women respect and all men equality.
When you die, let no one wish it had happened sooner.
They followed these daily and never knew they were poor.

Popcorn Sutton

Knock-kneed, bent double, twisted
as a coat hanger, hacking from a Lucky
that drips constantly from his lips,
Popcorn still scuttles crab-like around
his copper tubes, weighed down

by no concerns that plague us city folk
to death—mortgage payments, layoffs,
and boredom hanging like a shroud
of smog across any city's shoulders.
He has always known purpose and art.

Both drain from the spigot on his copper kettle
into Mason jars. After forty years, Popcorn
still makes the best moonshine I ever drank.
His truck veers only slightly from the paths
cut through Carolina brush by his father's father.

When corn prices went too high
and demand for untaxed liquor fell below the risk
of its production, when his sons switched
to curing cannabis and cousins sold their land
for housing tracts, Popcorn kept faith in our thirst.

Only the heartless forget heritage
to satisfy greed. At least that's what
he told me on my last trip south
and I respect a man who writes his own story
without regard for market value. Think

James Joyce in bib overalls, Pynchon with
a shotgun on his lap, or some barely read poet
the world never knows but is enlarged by each poem.

Cody's Diner

Wind hums lyrically and the moon springs over clouds
like one of those round dots dancing off words of a sing-along song
on the Mitch Miller Show, the only TV my father watches, singing along

as if the barbershop quartet's harmony might cancel the struggle to sell
one more car to some farmer who's saved the first dollar he ever made from
Cargill Grain Elevator. Tonight, Dad's brought me to the diner for dinner.

I'm twelve years old, wondering if exhaustion will finally kill me after
chasing time for years, as if it were a mugger, down some dimly-lit corridor
between the cowering buildings that line State and Main in the center of town.

Will each step become more desperate to discover if the effort's worth
the cost? I see the question unanswered in my father's eyes as he reads
the same menu he's had memorized all my life. I hear fatigue as he orders

or maybe a faint wish I'd walk home so he could slip around the corner,
enter Miller's Tavern, drink two martinis or five with the boys, play
gin rummy in the back room and talk about how the Cards should

climb from the cellar to win one pennant before he dies, one time, to prove
it can be done. Instead, we'll stay at Cody's Diner and he'll teach me how
to survive. The smell of his cigar smoke and Old Spice will fog my life

until I become a father and begin this process on my own. I'm talking
about wearing down from the friction of being the same person every day,
a drill bit bored in one beam of oak and then another until the metal frays.

Dancer

Sheena rises
like a church spire
during her flaming star
dance at the county fair
this hot July night.
The old men's howls swirl
higher and higher
as flame bursts
from her breasts, looping
into the audience
with a sizzle and pop.
Farmers duck, young boys
giggle, and Reverend Swanson,
camouflaged
in tee-shirt and ball cap,
thrusts both hands
into starched overalls, as if
squeezing his long sad
sigh upward.

We all hurl silver coins onstage
till the fire falls, the music grinds
down, and I recall
a hot July
many years before.
I loved Sheena then
when she was more than human,
and the mystery of her body
stoked my teenage dreams.

Life was simpler, sounded
like the rumble of straight pipes,
smelled of herbal shampoo
and baseball glove oil.
Nothing sagged,
not even my high school

batting average
or her eyelids heavy
with hemp.

This time it's different.
We face each other
with smiles that crack
the scars across our faces,
with stiffer gestures and slower
motion, with eyes glazed
in ceramic boredom,
with a need for balance
instead of grace,
I watch her cheeks burn
in lethargic yellows,
red heat banished
by the sense that what
we've both out stepped
for all these years
has made us one finally
and run us both to ground.

Note to Jill:

     I'm wearing the brown socks
you gave me.

They're beneath a table at the Mountainside Diner
waiting for me to half-eat half-cooked eggs
and wait, myself, for Rick.
He's the mechanic who swears
thirteen years of sobriety and promises
to fix my car, if he can just get the parts
from over the mountain before it snows, and if
those parts are the right parts, and if
State Farm Insurance mails the check, and if
his wife ever fixes him a warm meal, and if
his kids stop driving him crazy…

     Meanwhile,
Rick found me a nice room
in his brother's ski lodge (formerly the Route 9 Motel
before the repainting) at special non-skiing rates,
in case none of the above mentioned things occur this week.

The wall in my motel room (# 8) is thin,
like skin across the forehead that bleeds
profusely when hit with sharp objects, and for hours
my neighbors (# 7) throw
words against this membrane.
At 4am the screaming stops and the silence is terrifying.

     That's when
I put on these silly socks, walk to this diner, and order eggs.
Linda Ronstadt sings while I butter toast.
"Poor me. Poor me. Poor poor pitiful me."
The music reminds me how smooth
your small hands felt yesterday, the knuckles
like worry stones in my palm, how I miss you
flailing the pinball machine at Charlie O's

with those wondrous hips, how I've always wanted
to kiss the bruises the cold metal makes;
and then I think of places we might go together
in another lifetime, so I'm writing this note and wearing
these stupid socks that fit perfectly because
I have no other lifetime.

When the Stars Go Dark

There are no stars out tonight
in the alley behind Maidlow's liquor store.
Here, Charley Waters used to lean
against another old veteran of WWII
way back in the 60's when I'd come
down the block after high school
civics class and give him my allowance.
"You ain't old enough to drink," he'd say,
buying me a quart of Sterling beer and himself
a fifth of Thunderbird to quench his guilt.
They'd sip the wine, he and his buddy,
without saying a word, staring upward,
waiting for stars to pop through
the dusk like white kernels of kettle corn.

I'm in this alley decades later to piss
on the whitewashed wall and look
for those same stars. I've done it before
bought bourbon and snuck out here
even after Charlie died always to wonder
as those blooms, some ice and some fire,
flowered in the distant darkness
what Charley found in the vacuum
of the universe that caused
tears to swell in his glazed eyes.

I almost had it once when I first came home
numb from Vietnam—a shadow in the primal brain
forming a vague shape, gathering substance
as it seeped through me like hot tar—that
connection we've all had and lost
with our one beginning.

Tonight, it's possible to imagine again
when all that's above me is a black
well of overcast sky hung on nothing.

What connects us is our loneliness
tearing through the endless clouds,
arms outstretched begging the darkness
for a glimpse of those same stars
that always made Charley Waters cry.

II.

*War, what is it good for? Absolutely nothing.
Say it again...*
—Edwin Starr

Meditation on the Jungle Ambush

There were nights, long strands of time tied together with a thin wire of fear
when you could hear the full moon keening as it rose to wait for death.

Its only job was to end someone's loneliness forever by lighting
the path of a sniper's bullet or casting a dim shadow across a trip wire.

You wanted to believe it hung there to steer the tides receding at China Beach,
guide the course of a love you hoped to feel one day, capture the leap and swirl

of Basa fish or the unlocking of a Cac Dang flower, echo a tiger's growl
or a Black Kite's song, record the explosion of dew across the rice paddies.

Everything, even the hard click of brass as a round got chambered,
seemed more romantic and buoyant in the oblique and ductile glow.

In the end, all it did was burnish, and then not even from its own fire,
the monstrous clouds roiling above the banyan canopy overhead.

All it ever did was tempt you with its silent dusting of sugared light
to forget that each night ambush held the origin of your oblivion.

The VFW Rededicates the War Monument
On the Courthouse Lawn on Memorial Day

An honor guard from the local chapter, old men
bent from time, hard work, and memories, fires
a salute from even older rifles, seven times three.

Uniforms pressed and creased neatly,
They unfurl the flag and snap it in place above
the marble names carved at perfect attention.

The gestures crisp, the sun bright, the words
sincerely spoken all bring the crowd to tears.
A solitary trumpet sounds the final note of Taps.

The dead, not looking on from anywhere
and with no recall of why they died or why despite
their sacrifice the list grows longer, remain dead.

When a Zero Means Everything

Three hundred and eleven, 311, three eleven
like all numbers useful no matter how it's written.
It describes the number of chews you took
to swallow a piece of gristle on an overcooked roast,
defines the steps from your bed to the bathroom
as your prostate ages, lists the number of free cable
channels on the TV in your cheap motel room.
Three hundred and eleven may be the days after
your birthday or the days before Christmas.
Apart or together the digits mean nothing specific
and anything possibly depending on context.
They hold no guilt, anger, fear, or honor no matter
whispered or shouted, printed or scrawled.
But do this. Circle a zero in front of three
$$-0311-$$
at your Marine Corps recruitment office.
Then, the numbers are steps through a minefield,
rounds before the rifle jams, shadows at dusk,
seconds before air support, nights without sleep,
ways to lose a life, ways to take a life,
or a simple cue of how mankind can't quite
quantify its own value without dying.

Absence

I funneled them into single lines
at the roadblock on Highway One, patted
them down for rusty pistols, fuses
and trip wire that made this Tet
deadly for milk-faced Marines who stepped
off the wrong trail at the right time; but all
they carried inside them was fear, spitting out
fragments in chipped and broken slang.
"Beaucoup mal. Dien cai dao. Beaucoup mal."

A brown and stunning woman
appeared in my hands, as if pulled from a hat
or sculpted from clay and light. She shook
with panic and the taut spark
of her body jolted my cold circuits.
Then she was gone, running
south with a wave of refugees
toward the corrupt and declining China Sea.

The most beautiful person I ever touched

                ran from me.

She rushed past Buddhist monks,
past their temple doorways curling
with red dragons and snakes, past their
saffron robes swirling in the wind that spread
the blanched light of dawn, lifting it
and the scent of nuoc mam,
urine, and burned earth like incense
while Hue rose from a smoking horizon.

Tonight, as the sweat from some casual love
dries indifferently beneath a fan overhead
and I'm bored by the murmur
from the woman in the bed, I drift back

to that roadblock and that lilting, frightened voice,
to her blushing cheeks,
her thin lips, the slight white scar
beneath her left eyebrow,
to her hollow gaze and boyish breasts.
I feel her fingers, frail
yet resolute as a spider's web.
They wrap around my wrist, and shove
my soul away.
I want to taste the red wonder
of her tongue, draw
those onyx eyes across ten thousand miles
of death and into me. Instead,
I reach for my pants, curse when my car keys rattle,
slip from this motel, and dream
of making love to her
with what's left of love inside me.

Thirty Years from the TET Offensive

A car crashes and the Life Flight helicopter swoops so low
over the tree line, its black shadow clips the back of my head.
When I hear those turbines whine and rotors slap air with a rhythmic thud,
then Jim Morrison chants, "this is the end, beautiful end my friend…"
then my left knee aches for whiskey to dull the pain,
then I'm forced to drink beer warm, and eat powdered eggs cold,
then rain pours gray for several days, and those days fall down like rain,
then I can't sleep because someone pops the tab top on a Pepsi can,
slides a deadbolt home in the dark, bumps my bad leg, or steps behind me;
then summer sours the river, cypress molds and I smell fish rotting,
then the wind screams, the sky explodes, bone sears into red powder,
air fills my lungs like bits of broken glass, and those already dead
continue dying, charred slivers of wood and stone. Hell, thirty years
later I'm still hiding, nauseous and naked, in the napalmed jungle.

Translation

He's fourteen years old and already dead,
splayed on barb wire like a squirrel on a spit.
His mother leaves the burning joss stick inside
a roadside altar close by as she carries a basket
full of balut—those fermented duck eggs
women eat in the shell that strengthen a fetus—
to sell in the market place.

Time is too short for incidental grief in war.
You are young compared to her but old to death.
The smell of rotted flesh and moldy earth
no longer make you cringe as you rise
from the bunker, piss in a trough,
brush your teeth with brackish water, and listen
to her screams as if she were a peacock mating.

You load your rifle as the salmon colored sun melts
across banyan trees, as ghosts ascend from a heated mist
that floats above the rice paddies, as all thought dissolves
into the primal ooze of your survival. The woman wails
in language you don't understand or care to learn.
What you came to say has been spoken and what
she answers will take you years of pain to translate.

On Le La Street in Hue, 1968 & 2005

You were a package that came with this war, a bonus
like pound cake & peaches wrapped in C-rations on a good day.

The other marines outside the bunker didn't see your father
place an unlabeled box of condoms on the dirt floor or defiance
shading his black eyes as he surrendered your adolescence.

When my turn came I sold my watch to Marty Johnson for ten dollars,
market price for fresh flesh, and ticked off "I love you" in a brief stutter.

Each word has come undone, from wish to nightmare,
become the wet red bandana I placed across your eyes as propitiatory
blindness, a ransom sacrifice of sight for my shame.

Now, I've returned to Le La Street, stopped for white coffee
and to stare at the murals on this café wall. The jungle colors

rise in greens, browns, and yellows to reveal what hides
in the beige plaster—butterflies and naked children,
palm trees and elephant grass, rice paddies ringed in bamboo—

all some artist's optical illusion, like parts of you I see
mirrored in three young women leaning timidly on the bar.

Each one hopes that I might wave her over, knows I would
tip well, has learned that my appearance in this place of ghosts
proves my pockets weigh heavy with guilt.

Each table holds a vase of fresh Cac Dang flowers and the floor
has been swept clean as if your ghost expected my return.

The Holy Citadel in Hue, 1968 and 2008

1968: Smoke lifts the ash of bones
     from shredded flesh
     an offering to a purple sky

     A doxology of screams opens
     the mouths of mass graves wide
     and swallows smoldering children

     sacrificed by white phosphorus
     for the worship of the one true
     god constant with all men, War.

2008: Ghosts floating in fog
     trapped and waiting for mine
     to ride the mist that hangs

     over the Perfume River.
     I will join soon these left behind
     in the dark peace of the dead.

     Theirs, a quiet far less cruel than
     the cacophony of memory
     that sustains my aged sadness.

In Country, 1967

When I read this phrase in a Borges poem
"the desirable dignity of having died"
I thought of my friend Rick
sitting alone on that sandbag bunker
ten thousand miles from home his final day
in-country. He must have chosen
the cry of the black kite bird,
the stench of cordite, the sting of blood
on our last patrol together
beneath the bright blue sky of Hue
over winters in Kansas full of bad whiskey
and the guilt that grows in the soil of survival
as the best way to end an exceptional life
when he fired that round through his own brain
and eased his dread of leaving the dead behind.

The Memorial Wall

*Of what benefit to me is the multitude of your sacrifices?
says Jehovah. I have had enough of whole burnt offerings
and the fat of well-fed animals; and in the blood of young bulls
and male lambs and he goats I have taken no delight.*
—Isaiah 1:11

1. Arrival

You said Quang Tri was quiet when compared to Detroit
on Saturday night. I, being corn fed, believed you.
"Quiet as an old whore's bedroom," you said,
until the first whistle exploded and spilled
a mouthful of Tiger beer down my chin,
spraying the bolt on my new M-16. You grinned.

That smirk calmed all my fears
born in a place where ten seconds was a lifetime.
We lunged into a bunker when the next shell hit,
puppy clumsy. Like kids playing football,
chasing a fumble, we laughed, tumbling into darkness.

2. Halfway Home

Rice wine burned us both, but opium seared the marrow
from your boyish conscience.
Disappointed, you asked why I'd fired too far left.
The kid was pulling up his pants, an easy target
in the twilight. He reminded me of a robin I'd shot
with my BB gun, squatting, pecking the wet ground
unaware of my existence, or its own thin mortality.
I was ten then and crying.

Your smile froze after six months in that country,
hiding a heart hardened by a dozen firefights
and memories sewn into body bags.

Those eyes, glistening with assurance,
connecting us as brothers, barely flickered
through Thai stick smoke and a Dexedrine haze.
Reeking of white phosphorus and cordite,
you swore that only housecats killed for pleasure.

3. Short Time

It seems Monsoons came each day those last weeks
just to wash the blood away.
When our mortars hit the marketplace,
the barber's child died. Some stains
don't wash, like the memory of a sobbing man
whose only crime was cutting hair.

That's when I knew you were going home early.
The child's charred flesh made you unholy,
and the shortest distance from Vietnam to Detroit
was through blood atonement—your life for our sins.
When the shot popped, like a pricked balloon,
I realized you had fired it.
But, I screamed "Sniper" to the corpsman,
so your parents could be telegrammed—Hero—stop.
Prying the rifle from your suicidal fingers, I thought,
you should have squeezed the trigger, not jerked it.
A clean headshot, instead of my right palm,
could have closed your eyes.

4. Aftermath

We both flew home as casualties,
you in your coffin, me with my guilt.
You still deny me absolution
because you took the easy way back, Rick.
The dirt that covers your body now fills my mind.
Each time I reach for some liturgy
to chant, some Eucharist to swallow

to understand your sacrifice, to bring sanity
inside the empty sound of a spring rain, I gag.

Here, in my kitchen, drinking cheap whiskey
like my mom sent us years ago in shoe boxes,
I grasp for some boundary.
If only I could leave you there in Washington, D.C.
on a black stone scarred with carved letters
and the tears of your children unborn and unnamed.

Becoming the Dark

I have never been brave,
crying for hours at the loss
of Bambi's mother
and the death of Old Yeller.
Nightmares of flying monkeys
or the wicked witch's long nose
woke me for weeks after I saw
The Wizard of Oz in technicolor.
I must have missed twenty chances
to get laid during high school
terrified of females, and yet
I spent nights in war alone,
away from the safety of sand-bags
and concertina wire. I wandered
over trails paved in blood-red clay
behind and between thatch huts
that cross-hatched Highway One
south of Hue searching for something
near the rice paddies to elevate
my heart rate, flush my cheeks,
and stand hair up on my neck.
The idea of death was never far
from my mind, but the mind
is most fierce craving its addiction.
I would sit for hours, like a junkie
in an urban alley waiting for my fix,
back against the low cement wall
that ringed the old French schoolyard
and listen to whispers of the jungle dusk
as night was born from a day too small
to contain its immensity. First,
the trill of the toucans and the shrieks
of the monkeys. Then, a water buffalo
rustles against the snarl of a tiger.
The scent of pho and hint of lime
from the evening cook fires

sweep by with a hiss as the breeze
blows through the banyan trees
until a black sky quiets the stars.
In this darkness I become a god,
a beast without fear, a terrible force
waiting for moonflowers to open
and bloom in the shadows.

The Art of Deep Breathing

Because I loved brush strokes of blue air caressing the pink canvas
of my lungs I asked the supply sergeant for a rifle that worked.
Mine fired the first time and jammed. I was green, so he said, "No,
the Corps issues each jock strap one gun. Tough luck."
Outside the supply tent, I burned leeches off my left thigh.
The scent of Marlboros and scorched flesh sickened me. Thinking
of that fat sergeant, his two-beer ration, wrinkled Playboys, and warm tent,
I felt the cold night wind as it marched the rain along the Rockpile, down
from the DMZ. I hated how he stayed dry while I got wet.

Because I loved letters from Lynn Romer, molars grinding on cookies
mom mailed, pictures of sis in her prom dress, cheap perfume rising
from the local shopkeeper's neck, and a hot shower with real soap,
I asked the First Lieutenant to inspect my rifle. He squeezed off one round
at the Phu Bai rifle range. "Works fine boy. The problem's in your head."
"The casing won't eject, sir," I whined. "If I have to fire twice, I'm dead."
But he refused to listen. He said, " The first man up the hill's a hero."
I thought-the next one's a politician. From a foxhole, Armed Forces Radio
played Jimi—"Hey Joe, where you goin' with that gun in your hand."

Because I loved that swirl of orange flashing behind my eyes,
the adrenaline that embraced the art of deep breathing,
I took my broken rifle on patrol. I dreamed I saw one lieutenant
and one sergeant through my sights. At the right angle, a single shot
would do them both. Death by friendly fire is unavoidable in combat,
and no one questions a scared soldier with a broken rifle. Walking point, I
was an easy target filled with strange thoughts. If only I could have gotten
into a supply unit as an officer, I would be fat and fearless, breathing deep
and firing my rifle at nothing. I never wanted to kill anyone, anyway.
I just wanted to know I could.

March Is the Cruelest Month

Two robins and two jays trill
in counterpoint harmony as if Davis,
Coltrane, Parker, and Kirk flitted limb to limb
and spoke of various drugs and women
through the language of wind.

One leaf appears on a tree. You see it
through the bedroom window
and, like a caretaker in a cemetery,
sell yourself the illusion of rebirth
so you don't go crazy counting graves.

A woman is here and so are the stars,
full of cold fire lighting your mind
with memory and possibility.
The hooker on Tu Do Street
forty years ago with her silk ao dai

open to expose a thigh
the color of Tupelo honey reflected
these same stars from a different world.
You wonder briefly if that might be big
in some Jungian way, this woman lying so near

to your beating heart, a muscle you would
gladly tear from your chest and offer
as a mere token of what you feel,
like a ruby lifted from a velvet box, this woman
reminding you of how the past never

escapes the present, instead of vice versa.
It's always the subtle things, sandalwood
incense, the hiss of the teakettle on the stove,
the flicker of shadows along the candle-lit walls,
that flash the rocket round through your mind.

Then the room on Tu Do becomes the rubble
of your life. The dust and the cordite take away
your breath and the woman who no longer is
bleeds into the one you lay beside and love.
Then, you bury your face in her hair,
smell the lavender and your fear.

The Warrior's Elegy

The old lie: Dulce et decorum est, pro patria mori.
—Wilfred Owen

1. Agent Orange
   (for Joe)

In winter
the dead blow
where the wind goes:
through a cracked
window sill, beneath
an open coat collar around
a thick neck, behind
empty bleachers over
the football field, across
the Ohio river scarred
by the memory
of a speedboat's wake,
between the free weights
rattling at some brave
soul's out of season
yard sale, beneath the rising ping
of an engine with too many
miles and no warranty, the snap
of doubt in an all-weather American
flag and the strange cry of snow
spinning across a barren campus.

In winter
the wind blows
where the dead go,
shifting shadows into shapes
that terrify the living: a cemetery
of tulip stalks resurrected,
brought to attention and marched
at right angles to the ground,

shifting the weight of their dead
red helmets against the unbearable
burden of morning. Even the earth
can't hold the wind and keep it
quiet those first minutes
of dawn when it whines across
treetops and drop the sun.
Even the orange earth
trembles as the arc lights roar.

In winter
the wind belongs with the dead,
everywhere at once and nowhere at all.

2. VFW Post #1147
   (for Ron)

If I had backed my car from the garage this morning,
shifted to drive, aimed for Mrs. Taylor's Buick,
and pressed the accelerator to the floorboard,
then I would have been at war again because
war is my car wreck every day, seconds
slowing to hours as I close the hundred feet
between my bumper and her fender.
Metal crunching, glass flying, flesh ripping —
always good for mortality
checks and the illusion that soul is separate
from body. But I don't have the nerve for that kind
of action anymore. Instead, I drive
to the VFW, sit at the bar and wonder
when the seven rifles stacked
at attention in the wooden case might fire again. I wait
for the other old drunks to break ranks, stumble
from their stools, point the weapons skyward,
pierce the trumpeting of Taps with 21 sharp cracks
and the sweet smell of gunpowder.
In the end, dirt is all that gets shoveled over memories.
I remember Ron, those days we spent talking

about how Post Traumatic Stress Disorder was really
just the despair of living through the death of others,
how no one ever kills all the demons hidden
in the tree lines of his mind. Today I think of those
few words spoken by a Navy Corpsman fifty years ago
on a dirt trail a short distance outside Hue as he
bandaged my broken body. "Sometimes you know
a brother by the blood that runs through your veins
and sometimes you know a brother by the blood
that runs out of them."

Eating with Chopsticks in Vietnam

homme est ne' libre.
—Rousseau
homme est ne' poltron
—Conrad

An art not easily mastered,
or so I learned when the village elders led my squad
beneath the tiled roof of the French schoolhouse
and fed us cahn cho in wooden bowls.
We rinsed it down with red rice wine
in the noon heat of the Lunar New Year
and I mastered the art before the meal ended.
Laughing, I balanced one grain
between those two sticks of wood while the air filled
with sweat and ginger, while the sniper steadied
his rifle in the fork of a rubber tree.
Marty pointed at my success and giggled like a child
who saw the wonder in a rose petal for the first time
before he dropped face first into the scalding duck soup,
as if the sniper's bullet had pried open a small door
above his eyes, crawled in, and flicked the switch off.
In that split second I could have painted substance
for a shadow, written a book that breathed, sculpted
a living form from marble, or composed a score in silence.
I was supernatural, a Jeremiah in jungle boots who watched
the world's future disappear between the rice on the wood
and Marty's blood and bone on my face like wet sand.
Then I ran for cover and hid behind a chipped stone wall.

At The Museum of Modern Art
in New York City I Wondered:

Suppose Van Gogh shot himself
in the foot with a rifle, rather than sliced
his ear with a carving knife? Would he be
an artist, or like my friend Williams,
who listed left and limped?

Williams doesn't know Van Gogh,
unless that was the name of the opium dealer
we found on a back street in Saigon.
But, there's not much difference between them.
Both had beards, red hair, and strange visions
of a world gone mad.
Their eyes saw shades of blue and hues of red
swirled in paranoid pools of color.
Williams drew graffiti on the concrete walls in Hue,
sold his watch for a blow job in Phu Bai,
laughed as nuoc mam ran over his chin like barbeque sauce,
sobbed when the amphetamines were gone,
placed the barrel of an M-16 against his own foot
and squeezed carefully, as if the trigger would bruise his finger.

After the medics carried him away,
I saw him one last time at Leavenworth Prison,
where the Army sends self-inflicting soldiers.
I visited on a Sunday. He never spoke,
but as this self-portrait of Van Gogh,
stared wildly over my head afraid
of closing his eyes.

On the Streets of Saigon in the 21st Century

After reading a U.S. court decision finding the makers of Agent Orange not responsible for birth defects in Vietnamese children

They swarmed me like hummingbirds,
a flock of boys two generations from war
and twitching so fast in the white sun I hardly saw
the animated hunger hiding in their dark eyes.
With watches and postcards held aloft,
some scuttled on skateboards while others
scraped kneepads and bike gloves
along Dong Khoi Street dragging knapsacks
full of salvaged treasure, Zippos, rings,
bullet jacket brass, photos, and private things
torn from battle dead thirty years before
these casualties were ever born.
Their humid voices echoed over traffic
and claxtons from cargo ships moored
or dry-docked in the Bason shipyard.
I bought a pack of 555's from tiny twins,
maybe twelve years old, maybe fifty.
The acrid smoke veiled the stench of dead
fish rising from the Saigon River as the whole
group hailed a cyclo driver for my ride to peace,
my reason for return, a ceremony by the Ministry
of Arts and Literature, an invitation to remember,
a celebration of repentance and forgiveness.
Each child waved goodbye as if we were cousins,
ordinary people with ordinary lives.
Some used their only hand, those without arms
shook their feet, three wriggled fingers attached
to legs, one whose torso was backward turned
away and gave me a hug. The twins, fused
at the ears, smiled a bizarre double grin
born from three chipped and blackened teeth.

Operation Lancaster, 1967

1.

You notice the small things first,
the smell of Sterno-heated C rats,
sweat-rotted jungle boots, and dead water
in the rice paddies. The blanched sun
opens its mouth over the rubber trees
and swallows the last black bite of night.
The metallic trill of a jungle bird
you've never seen
hammers morning into your head
like a ten-penny nail.
Phuc Tran's rice wine still burns
through the roof of your mouth.
You haven't even raised
yourself from the hole you slept in
before a dragon fly whizzes by with a sound
like why, the single word, that one small word
that brings all these small things into focus
and makes the dawning greater
than the sum of its parts.

2.

Death is buried where you piss and who knows
when the trembling wind will stop. Maybe
the mist foaming from the mourning earth
or the flesh-colored dust soaking through
your flak jacket will shield your heart and lungs
from the jagged burn of hot metal. Maybe not.

Small beige people glide by on bikes and scooters.
Some wave across the concertina wire
and you wave back as if the wire were not
an ocean, as if you might not have already drowned

them all in your numbed mind. That same sound
whizzes by, louder now than the dragon fly.

3.

So motion is life, you think,
the fuel that fires your green age,
the clack of a rifle bolt
sliding home,
elephant grass churning
like the jade sea at China Beach,
the flutter of your butterfly heart
as it brushes against your ribcage,
the jangle of the wind chimes
on a sentry's watchtower
and the earth spinning so fast on its axis
that you get dizzy when Sergeant Williams
signals the patrol out past an old French
schoolhouse scarred by white phosphorus.

So motion breeds death, you think,
the force that shoves itself into your throat
from some ancient era of your back brain,
the uncontrollable twitch in your left eye,
and the slight palsy of your trigger hand.
You stutter in your step
as you push through the bamboo
to see the whirling point man deconstruct,
spun round, lifted up, pulled apart
by the mine beneath his feet.
You point and fire at shadows
till the shadows shoot back and screams
knead themselves into one long knot
of sound devoid of cause.

4.

You caress your dead like baby birds fallen
from their nests too young to fly.
You bundle them gently into rubber bags
and tag their toes so families will know them.

But who knows the other dead?
Who cares enough to bury him,
a boy of twelve,
asking why he lies in a pool of brackish mud
stained orange with blood and urine.
Where is his ball glove and Yankees cap?
Who sees his parents shrink over an altar,
lighting sandalwood joss sticks, whispering
mantras that resurrect only smoke?

When you squeezed your trigger and the bullet
punched through the tight jungle air to touch
his chest, did you hope for his death
to be part of something bigger?

You still notice the small things first:
Sweat that stings your eyes while you wait
for the blue cloud of cigarette smoke to ignite
your lungs and a whisper like why
as the boy's last breath rushes past his small lips.

On Veterans Day a Vietnam Veteran Reads
the Names of American Soldiers Killed in the Iraqi War

At first, it's about getting through an anonymous list—
Bill Jackson, Robert Johnson Jr., Mike Jones, etc.—
and holding the microphone close enough to your lips
so the clang of barge bells on the river behind you don't
drown the syllables drifting like unmoored buoys
through the current of moist air in this commerce of life.

The sparse crowd bows a collective head, flags pop, traffic
hisses and slows beside the monument. In the middle of the list
syllables animate your past. Blood pumps through scrawled
letters as if loops and lines were blue veins. Names play baseball,
watch movies, walk hand in hand with teenaged lovers.
You'll never meet any of these men and yet you know them all,

perfect bodies ripped apart, reappearing for a moment,
disappearing whole in the blankness of the turning page.

Peace

A small green fruit grows
only from the earth in Hue. Seeded
by the Trai Va tree, it rises round
and moist in soil blood-red with memories.

I share it now with my friend
Vo Que at the Garden Café
just off a dirt trail in this city where
my heart stopped singing
so many years ago, silenced
in a battle to claim what was never mine.

Que and I are two poets grown old
by sharing one dream from different worlds.

Here, in this jungle heat beneath lavender
blossoms and banyan trees that once shaded
tanks, rifles, mines, and death,
we speak of life. A voice within
us both chants in counterpoint harmony
beyond our separate tongues. Sometimes,
it makes the rustle of a spring rain,
the cry of geese in the gray dawn,
the whistle of wet wind through bamboo,
the drum of the Perfume River
beating ceaselessly on the stones of shore.
Sometimes, it whispers like a child's smile
or sunrise cracking a robin's egg sky.

I have traveled ten thousand miles,
decades through tormented time
and shattered space to hear
this voice rise within me once more,
to share a simple meal
with my friend, who, like the Trai Va,
no longer bears me malice for crimes
committed in my youth.

III.

Being Irish, he had an abiding sense of tragedy, which sustained him through temporary periods of joy.
—William Butler Yeats

Dinner at Lorenzo's

A bow-tied waiter counts wine bottles in racks stacked strategically
behind the bar. Vines crawl along murals, light switches,
and spackled walls. Fresh bread bakes in the oven. Its scent kneads
into olive oil and oregano. Soft jazz trills in time with the ceiling fan
that needs a new bearing. A good Tuscan red sweeps across my tongue
like a velvet broom. I should be thrilled, but the limp of the glazed chef
carrying lamb as gently as a child lost to war, the absence of love
in a man's eyes when his hand closes over his lover's hand,
and the dazed smile of the hostess who wants to write pretty poems,
remind me that suffering idles in us all, a cosmic engine that torques
one scream above the howls of thousands, revved, waiting to rend
our helpless words into flayed shreds of desperate stardust. One breath
or a vague need slips it into gear. We all bear the drive like the taste
of this expensive meal, overcooked and doused with too much salt.

My Shame in 1958

Elmer Lucas paced the streets of my small town
with a grand impatience for everyone in his way.

A light-skinned black man, tall and wispy, his face long
and stubborn as a mule's, he shouted "Fuck you" to us

if we dared to meet his glare and held tightly the arm
of his sister whom he raped often and beat to miscarriage.

We knew nothing of crimes, his or ours, in pre-pubescent days.
Elmer seemed less than human by virtue of his Tourette's

and a lack of proper deference towards us as the privileged sons
of white men. I did not understand the cruelty of humans then

and when we called him names just to hear him curse our mothers,
I laughed as loudly as my pals at the innocent pleasures of our games.

Art of the Deal

Walt Whitman sells Volvos these days.
Though "Song of the Open Road"
seems meant for leather soles and dirt trails,
rolling hills and green prairies, blue skies
and free-wheelin' back-slappin' pipe smokin'
suspender flapin' apple pluckin' cherry
pickin' days of spontaneous laughter,
Old Walt's literary caretakers find it more
useful as a selling point since art is measured
by cash in the bank in this electronic age.
All you need is a television screen
a simple juxtaposition of words and context,
a handsome hipster with a laptop drinking
coffee in one of those lonesome road diners
"off the beaten path" and full of bohemian
imagery, and then add a waitress
with too many teeth in her smile.
Have her ask a question that means nothing
to either one of them—say like, "whatcha
writing" followed by a cryptic response
"don't know yet" as if someday he might.

 —Flash forward two seconds—

The song of the open road sings with the sound
of rubber over asphalt and the rich baritone
of some movie star you think you know
but can't quite remember as a car that costs
more than an Ivy League education roars by.
The same hipster steers and the narrator steals
Whitman's soul. This is the new America,
the avant-garde art of the deal.
We all sit back and smile at the TV screen
our hearts overwhelmed with a glow
of cultured joy and remark to whomever
may think we're smart, "Isn't that a poem

from somewhere?" without realizing what
we've just bought and who has been sold.

South of Atlanta on I-75, I Find America

Those rotting pear-shaped people
with their sunken chests and flesh flowing

like a feral river over the shores of wide belts,
each one with so many chins the weight of them

drags the thin-lipped mouth open in perpetuity,
I see them everywhere today, at truck stops, rest areas

as they walk tiny poodles with spiked collars,
in flea markets full of Civil War-flagged peanut brittle.

They offer me no apology for their misshapen shirts
and I offer none for my unkind and unfair thoughts,

or the foul mood their appearance puts me in
now that I've stopped at an all-you-can-eat buffet.

It isn't that I have no pity for the gluttony I see
as the crowd of two-footed cattle rustle around

a mountain of fried chicken and a sea of gravy,
or fear, as I instinctively pat my own sagging belly.

This tragedy of corpulence isn't personal. Well,
maybe a little personal since we all appear related.

Mostly, it's metaphorical and that's where my anger
ruminates, at the point where something is

what it is not and something is not what it is. This
crowd of fat cousins has become my country, a swarm

of pasty people blanched even more by the prospect
of losing their place at the dining trough. Pushed aside

by the largest and their horrible hunger, those left behind scratch to keep crumbs away from bus boys.

There's a Lesson for Us on the Perfume River

Litchi leaves, mangosteens, orchids, and flame trees
carried on an August breeze are offered to the river,
whose name is the fragrance rising from it in early fog.
The woman's movements sing an ancient song as ageless
as her parchment face in honor of the river's name.
Beneath the woven blanket of bamboo, she lights a fire,
boils her breakfast tea, and then loads a small boat
with baskets of colza, cabbage, fennel, and peppers
grown in a fertile soil that bonds her soul to those
who came before and those who will come after.
Her frame, twisted by work and time, begins to pole
the boat through shallows. Bare feet keep a drum beat
stern to bow and bow to stern for the music of toucans,
black kite birds, and all the shrill harmonies alive
in jungle banyan trees. With a slow current, she
takes this trip to market while children harvest rice
along the river bank, while the sun spreads across
Hue, the Purple City. Her bare feet keep a drumbeat
bow to stern and stern to bow while men pull their nets
of basa fish to shore through the four Chinese eras,
the defeat of Kublai Khan, the slavery of the French,
and the slaughter of her children by the Di bo Chet.
Not once in two millennium does she ask her god
about the horror of being and the horror of going on.

Posse Commitatis from Standing Rock—Winter, 2016

My father, a war hero, was born on May 4th
and if alive today would be ninety-five years old.
A staunch Republican and defender of all things
red, white, and blue, he rarely questioned
the leaders of his free world or the need for law
and order. But, he always felt ashamed
on that one birthday in May when soldiers
rushed a line of Kent State students and shot
four dead because they refused our newest war.
That was almost fifty years ago and it's a winter
morning, not a May afternoon. Yet, this thought
clouds the daybreak, the crinkle of fresh frost
in my footsteps toward the barricade, the pine
scent entwined with cinnamon, a dusting of snow
& the crystalline rays of sunlight strung
like spider webs across the sky and into the bluff
above the bridge of North Dakota Highway 18.
It has to do with an idea never changing substance
even though the form of its delivery does,
police behind rifles and bayonets armed to fight
a war against people they took an oath to protect,
an engine of profit that powers a Congress,
the division of ideals by color and gods, farm lands
that lie fallow for cash while children go hungry,
the murder of virtue through the loss of art.
I once saw a Buddhist bonze soak his saffron robe
in gasoline and light himself on fire, a statement
that death was preferable to uncontrolled desire.
My father did not believe in self-immolation
for a whole nation, but he would concede,
I'm sure, that history has wasted its breath on us,
that a fog of ancient fears is waiting to be burned
alive by the rituals of power meant to bank the flames.

An Ordinary Man Goes Shopping at Kroger's

no more to use the sky forever but live with famine and pain a few short days
—Robinson Jeffers from "Hurt Hawks"

Between the basmati rice and the garbanzo beans
an urge for chaos nested in his brain waiting
to hatch a scream. What drove this need
that would embarrass him and frighten shoppers?
Was it the woman who dropped the ketchup bottle
and left the floor bleeding or his own image
in the angled mirrors above the shelves?
Reflection is the mirror's way of dreaming.
Once he dreamed a white tiger in Vietnam, a sign
his whole patrol claimed was only fog until the roar.

From the seafood aisle the stench of fish forced him
to the produce section. Even there, the sweet scent
of overripe Kiwis and organic oranges felt tragic
in a feral wake of swarming fruit flies and housewives.
The idea of screaming filled his mind
with inner consistency. He could prove
all that he believed, and believed
all that he could prove. When does the habit
of pretending faith become the habit of faith?

>   *Intoxicated*
>   *Trees list left*
>   *When they drink the wind*

He had a student who wrote haikus and joined the army.
Her favorite poem they read in class was "Hurt Hawks,"
she confessed in an email from Iraq on the same day
shrapnel severed her spinal cord. The memory among
a group of teens hoping to buy a case of beer
paralyzed the anger in his throat. Hushed by her smile,
he filled his cart with cottage cheese and frozen dinners.

What is left over
Is carried
In math and in life

A stirring in the ancient sea, where he had come from nothing and all, where the currents connected him to life before and after time, brought him a gift that kept him whole, a single line from her favorite poem.

Elegy for Charles Darwin

on the 150th Anniversary of The Origin of Species
and During the Trial of Faith Healer Dale Neuman

He reasoned we'd evolve,
become greater than the sum of our parts,
but Darwin never met Dale,
who killed his daughter with prayer
because doctors are devils.

He conjectured we'd adapt
from the inside, like Stop Leak,
and plug the holes in our lives,
bar our souls from oozing out,
check ignorance from seeping in.

Darwin surmised we'd adjust
to our futures, but Dale didn't like
this new century full of free will,
science minus magic, and no gods left
to exorcise his daughter's diabetic demons.

Dale prayed, injecting spirit instead
of insulin and for his faith, his prayers
were answered. A coma cured the child
and sent her back to Jesus, a home where
Darwin's evil is barred from entry.

Suicide in High School

My friend Sue perched
on the rail of Severn's Bridge,
dog-eared and faded copy
of the Tom Robbins' novel
Even Cowgirls Get the Blues
stuck behind her belt buckle.
She freed her white-knuckled grip
on the metal cross beams, spread
her arms and let the fringes
of her brown buckskin jacket
unfold like feathered wings. Then,
she left the boundaries of earth,
rising just slightly at first
as if the light spring breeze might
lift her to orbit the stars slung
so close to those cold girders.
We watched in awe, a small group
of classmates passing a joint.
Some cheered her amazing aplomb.
Others, myself included,
realized as she spiraled
into the river below
the absolute gravity
of believing all birds are free
beyond the chains of the sky.

Plumber's Hymn # 1

Sunday morning. Bells peel salvation
from the tight grasp of the last work week.
My neighbor's backyard chickens peal along
in harmony unaware they are being saved

for some heavenly future dinner.
I shuffle by the Baptist church as doors
swing open spilling the fresh cream of Jesus
onto the sidewalk—children with mothers in tow,

fathers with Bibles tucked under arms, brightly clad
couples newly cleansed of sexual sin and clinging
to a dream of paradise in another world if only
they can keep from any pleasure in the current one.

I wonder as I wander, do these righteous
know the plumber I called yesterday to disembowel
a drainpipe in my kitchen sink. As he wound the cable
downward into a hell of garbage that blocked the flow

from my faucet, he spoke of his own salvation, how
his kids had no gratitude for his nonspecific sacrifice,
how the government denied his disability claims
because he could still work even though his back hurt.

Jesus got him right through prayer during the foreclosure
on his home and his divorce. Jesus led him to a doctor
and his oxycodone. "Jesus," he said, would soon unclog
my pipes if I prayed hard enough and kept the water

running freely. He was on his knees already, would I join
him for a chance at grace? His faith gave me hope,
and I considered supplication for a moment, perhaps a trip
to this very church and then, I saw the cost.

Collateral Damage

Marge leans against air.
It's the one solid object in her life.
She rides to a hospice and reads
the news each day to her vegetative son,
his face unchanged through her litany
of genocides fratricides riptides pedophilia.
"We're all collateral damage in God's design,"
she says at least twice a week. "It's the price
we must pay for being human."

We're waiting on number 19,
a new eco-friendly bio-diesel bus
the mayor claims will reduce carbon footprints.
It's late this morning and a plump school girl
bums a smoke from the gardener whose car
got swallowed by the bank. With his footprint
already gone, he needs a ride to a new job
and she's been banned from the school bus
for terrifying small children with her adolescence.
I search for headlights in the predawn dark,
enduring this street corner, unable to admit
what we all fear, that time lost
is one way misery gets measured.

For me, god's plan remains elusive,
the cost too high for my faithless budget.
The good seems neither greater nor patterned,
more circumstance than intent. Like roulette
it traps us in some relentless hole where
we bear random wounds in solitary confinement
as the spin of the wheel wears down
and sometimes allow ourselves a state of grace,
as the boy I saw in Bosnia playing basketball
on one leg, the other blended with the scree
of a minefield where he attended school once,
or as these people waiting at this bus stop
who suffer silently the ache of unearned despair.

Anniversary

Mom lays sockeye salmon
rolled in cracker crumbs
into a lake of hot lard as Saltines
swim along the cast iron skillet's shore.

She smiles at the browned flesh
of the burned fish my father hates
eating, but will as a small sacrifice
for his indiscretions with Beefeater's gin.

This is love: fifty years of marriage
without the sin of murder,
betrayal rationed by shot glass.
This is sacrifice: fifty years sharing
six rooms furnished with fear that one
might outlive the other and be left alone.

The Pursuit of Knowledge

It begins by counting ceiling tiles during a lecture on fossils.
Semouria is a reptilomorph named for a town in Texas.
Winged lizards nested on the ground, unlike bats.
Straight-ankle thecodants evolved into crocodiles,
then humans.

I'm learning these facts because I want to become
a civilized man. In fact, I knew a thecodant
in Okinawa with perfect ankles.
Her neck smelled like jasmine and vanilla.
For an extra dollar, she whispered the name of my first love
when I climaxed. I think I chose Karen.

"Anapsid, synapsids, and diapsids may have been warm blooded."

The professor's voice flutters along the walls,
a disconnected shadow in fluorescent light
and the girl sitting in the chair next to me is warm,
is no fossil. She smells like honeysuckle,
her hair, the laces of vines in my mind
that must be gently parted to reach a thought.
Her sighs distract me. They sound like spring rain
kissing a small lake.

"Vocalization among different groups of dinosaurs
would strongly suggest some kind of social interaction."
.
Beside the blackboard, the professor chants his mantra.
I hear the NVA in the streets of Hue
during Tet of '68 before their immolation.
I smell the cordite still and feel the heat
from the tracer rounds we marched up the pavement
in perfect cadence with the screams.

"Some cataclysmic event ended their reign over earth
and all we have left are fragments of their bones."

I'm learning to keep some knowledge from myself,
pretending, as it creeps back into my consciousness,
I'm someone else, an actor in a play
inspired by neither character, nor plot as much
as the numb vacancy in my own voice and my skill at being
what I'm not, perfectly.

Blurbing

A man named Gary wrote a story
about a war we both fought
in different parts of the same jungle.

Instead, it turned out to be about how anticipation kills us.

Once he finished all the writing
and the story got bound in a book,
Gary wanted a famous writer to blurb the back cover.

You know, pen a clever review that points to brilliance within.

Sadly, all Gary got was me.
I liked his story, not in a moral
or tasteful or happy-ending sense,

but rather in an obscene and honest war is fucked-up sense.

Gary thought my blurb fit sort of well,
like a cheap suit that he might wear
to a wedding or a cousin's funeral,

but he couldn't say how the blurb
made him feel because
he just wanted it to be over.

You might think that Gary meant the business with his story being over.

He didn't.

He was tired.
He couldn't eat.
He couldn't sleep.

The past that crippled Gary was the present.
Waiting for a death that happened decades ago is exhausting.

Eli's Elegy

I don't waltz or tango
fly the fly or jerk the jerk,
shimmy,
bop,
twist,
or cha-cha when the jukebox
flays the air with music
in some bayou dive, when
something inside
wants to dance its way out.

      But, Eli did
with a wide grin for all the years
we spent drinking gin, his gold
tooth refracting the dim bar light
hoping to catch a bar maid's eye
or perhaps the promise of a kiss
to ease the sadness of last call.

I can't cry either
even though his memories
have killed him finally.
We all die from the guilt of living.
He made his choice
and was made by it when we
came home from 'Nam.
He shot his wife through the head
as she lay in bed with her lover.

I will cry once, though
and I will dance the next time
I hear his favorite
song *Bon Ton Roulet* in some
Cajun juke joint near the swamps
that he loved—wild fiddles
howling in the blue moon night,

zydeco's expelling a last spasm
of laughter at my twirling
drunken shadow—Yes,
I will dance, stumble, and cry
into a new dawn knowing no man
is the man he believed he was.

     All those years
in prison the rage seeped
from his heart and his parole
became a weight of shame,
impossible to carry with the truth
that the dead are never really dead
except to themselves.

Oakland Park Cemetery, Atlanta
On a Sunday Morning in June

Magnolias bloom bitter white
in silent sunlight.
Around their frail arrogance
purple hydrangeas bow in submission.
There is no breeze as I hold the same ground
General John B. Hood held watching
while Sherman burned his beloved city.

The scent of lavender hovers above
rows of blanched gravestones
like the sickly sweetness of cotton candy
after the carnival has left the midway.
The stones stand at attention, an army
of cold marble behind Hood's cenotaph
that leads them in battle to meet the last enemy.
But here there is no sound of trumpets
no King and angels to conquer Death
only brittle bones and flesh gone to seed
in the red Georgia clay.

It was said the light of battle shone in Hood's eyes,
that he believed in cause, cross, and crown.
But, I choose to think the brightness more
a sign from flames reflected on his Quixote face,
a keen awakening that one day all the marrow
of his warriors would mingle with the dust
of his slaves buried in the plots next to theirs,
Hood's tall and thin shadow cast over them all.

Between Nogales and the Border

Prickly Pear cactus is born
as gunmetal blue fades to gray.
This remains of darkness—the decaying earth
shadows of tumbleweeds and in a soft breeze,
an echo of the world laughing. One coyote
stretches across the asphalt as an early morning
offering to the god of diesel. The beast
was slaughtered on a singular and suicidal
search for a need that will always remain
unknown—even to the coyote, especially to him.
A blue whale's song sounds at a thousand leagues.
A train whistle carries one hundred miles.
How far does the sound of death carry?
It's a fair question given how slowly
time passes through the mind that suffers.
When this coyote stood paralyzed by headlights,
the line on the road hypnotic in his eyes
like a yellow cobra swaying to the flute song
of metal, tires, and then despair, a misery
of which coyotes are mostly unaware arrived
as the hint of an unknown hunger: no more
sweet scent of desert rain, fire of falling stars,
joy of scratching for fleas or lazy stretches
in the morning sunlight, no more to see a feather
float upward or hear leaves rattle over dry sand.
The glitter, like broken glass, gone from his eyes
at the last glimpse of all he loved.

At a Small Mexican Diner

I once saw a mule in Matamoros,
a fine case of pastoral heterosis,
more strength than the donkey, more
pluck than the horse, smarter than either.
No species of its own, this offspring
of Equus caballus and Equus asinus,
though sterile, proved an upgrade of both.
But irate at its braying, his owner rose
from dinner with no interest in what caused
the mule's cries, only the nuisance,
and as the sun set he shot the thing
through the head. I can't forget the sight
of that mule left to rot in dust and heat,
flies blanketing the black blood
in the unpaved street, nor how slight
the bother involved in killing
as the man returned to his meal
without even washing his hands.

My Childhood Is Dead—Long Live My Childhood

Time's sovereign. It rides the backs of names cut into marble. And to get back, one must descend, as if into a mass grave. —Larry Levis

On cloying winter weekends when school was closed
mom bundled me against a wind so hostile to the skin
red cheeks burned as if scratched by a thousand thorns.
She sent me out to play with all the neighbor kids
while she laundered, scrubbed, and baked, as did each
neighbor mom. Dad spent his time away from work
working in the garage, working on the snow-filled
black and white TV, or working with the landscape,
as did each neighbor dad who lived the American dream.
Old Ike had promised every family that TV,
along with two cars, a picket fence, low mortgage rates,
processed food, dial phones, and a prosperous peace.
We ignored the cruel whiteness of his pledge
because we were white.

The movie house offered Saturday matinees,
the incense of freedom and the shelter of fantasy.
Here, I congregated with grade school friends.
Bug-eyed in 3-D glasses and screaming, we warmed
our blood dodging arrows and Indian ponies that rode
across the plains, out of the screen, and over our heads.
The pasty face of Tom Mix, his Stetson as bleached
as his face, his six guns blazing and Indians falling,
taught us the color of goodness. The sweet tang
from Dum-Dum suckers distracted us long enough
not to question when the old usher, wig askew,
forced black kids away from the water fountain
up the stairs to a secret place called "balcony."

Fifty years have passed since I first stuck a piece
of Wrigley's Spearmint to the bottom of a seat so I could
kiss a girl named Pam while Elmer Fudd stuttered his way
through my self-conscious pubescence. When I got married,

some corporate Mega-Plex partitioned the main floor
into four separate screens without the vision of a future
where memory and imagination, fractious children
that they are, might play trapped in a world
full of cell phones and iPads outside its doors.

Now, my children are grown, my parents buried,
I'm driving past the movie house one last time.
The marquee's busted, the doors are sealed with plywood,
a wrecking ball is swinging from the arm of a crane,
and the hint of stale popcorn rushes in the car's window.

Sunday Morning Synchronicity

The worshipers of lenient gods guide
their boats from ramp to river's edge
till the brown Ohio becomes a palette,
a rainbow of mud and diesel fuel.
In go Liquid Asset, Miss Behavin', Bite Me,
Wet Dream, Hydro Therapy. What better way
to serve on Sunday than glide along
with Jesus in a wake of sunlight across
the foam of jet skis beneath heavenly sky.
The current swirls in joy along the cutbank
and the holy hum of outboards harmonize
with the squeals of dreams that ride the waves.
These aquatic conquistadores do not see,
or if they do, do not care to acknowledge,
a pickup truck along the levee road
as it separates bicycle from rider
and returns them both to earth in a knot
of steel and flesh. Even if a vague shiver
drifts like the mist from a passing barge
along their spines, this random sacrifice—
this propitiatory misery—is forgotten
with the next deep breath.

Breakfast at Denny's

1.

Inert in the middle
of sizzle and splash,
I am an audience of one
for the bebop jazz
of thumping sandals,
sliding chairs, flapping
wallets, the cow-bell clang
of a bad bearing
in the solitary ceiling fan,
the rattle of a sports page
and a tickling spoon
across the keyboard of one
nearly empty coffee cup,
a melody that pauses when
the woman at the next table
chews her unbuttered toast
with her eyes closed.

Fermata.

2.

If you could comfort any person
who chokes down a grand slam breakfast,
it would be the man in the Boy Scout shirt.
Coffee in hand, his rheumy eyes stare
at the reflection in the glass window.
If it's true that memory is the destroyer
of dreams then he must be terrified
watching, waiting for the present to pass.
It's not the filthy blond disheveled hair,
the twisted lips and purple gums or chewed
fingernails that scrape his scarred chin,
not the torn boots or crusted khaki pants

worn to a final sheen that drive you
to an opposing wall so much as the stench
rising from his soul and the talk he's having
with his own insane image. You want to help
but won't come close enough to hear the words
for fear they might infect you with his disease.
All you can do is marvel at how easily
everyone pretends he isn't really there.

The English Professor Reflects on Career Choices

He not busy being born is busy dying.
— Bob Dylan

My friend Matthew stuffs dates with goat cheese and bakes
delicacies from countries with names I can't pronounce.
We are having a party. I laugh, drink gin, and say
to no one in particular, "It doesn't get better that this."
I heard that cliché an hour before I got here. A truck driver
whispered those words to some indifferent waitress
he attempted to impress with an erudite air
and a dollar bill he handed her for some burnt coffee.
Fading into the diesel-driven night, his shadow limped after.

I wonder which of us is more sincere or if irony matters.
We've both spent our lives hauling someone else's freight
over miles of chopped up highways, hopped up on caffeine,
loneliness, and hungry at the wrong times for the wrong things.
When life smells like gasoline and cheap perfume, does it matter
which road we take is paved with asphalt or which with ideas?

Elegy for a Postal Worker

When you scrub china
in hot dishwater and remember
Brenda, it's not because
you ever saw
her in the kitchen
in the ten years you carried
mail together, stopping
for lunch at Metzger's Tavern,
laughing as your separate dreams
of doing great things were reduced
to fried bologna sandwiches
and stuffing utility bills
in strangers' mailboxes.

The clink of dishes
and the clatter of spoons,
the hiss of the faucet
and the squeak of a towel
across clean glass—the sounds
you'd expect her home to make
if she were in it—and the scent
of lilac soap as it used to wash
the air on those mornings you hid
behind the convenience store,
remind you of who she was
by what she wasn't.

When the cancer hid in Brenda's breast
and nested there, she phoned.
What do you say
to someone who knows
she's dying and can't hide from it?

How do you hide from her funeral?
Maybe something comes up, a trip to the dentist,
a TV show, a new job offer, laundry,

the guilt from knowing that though you were older
and maybe less worthy, it would be you
and not her who sent flowers.

Free Market Enterprise

Outside my sister's country home five wild turkeys
stretch worms out of black dirt, strut, and flex their wings
as if the sky might suddenly free them from its gray weight.

A doe and two fawns graze on the patchy grass of spring,
nudge the birds aside to search for more, and freeze in place.
I think the squawks and flutters have alarmed the deer,

caused them to rethink their actions, but I can't be sure.
No sound echoes through the bay window. The kitchen,
like space, is a vacuum separating me from the world.

Then, it comes, a buzz saw with legs and teeth,
seething drool and hackled backs, a pack of wild dogs
with no regard for harmony, only personal hunger

and the need to feed that has fermented in their bellies
from a time beyond time, a prehistoric urge that separates
beasts from mere animals and proves evolution has its limits.

In an instant, the deer have fled, the dogs have savaged
two turkeys beneath a copse of oaks and maples.
The rest, a gaggle of feathers and fear, beat the air senseless

until, unable to rise above the chaos, they ignore it
and return to their harried search for earthworms.
Hunger has purified their souls.

IV.

The knife came down, missing him by inches, and he took off.
—Joseph Heller

A Balancing Act

Son House is on the radio.
The old Delta bluesman belts out a chorus
from "John the Revelator" acapella and drunk.
The words sound crystalline and prophetic,
like the timbre of a bell in perfect pitch.
Once House passed sixty, he had to be spoon-fed
the right amount of whiskey before he sang.
Too little and the words disappeared, too much
and they reappeared in shapes of unrelated meaning.
His mind sought balance, not between vague concepts
such as good and evil but the steadiness of memory
that creates a self, substance in a song beyond its form.
It never really mattered that he drank to find it
only that it flowed, like a river springs from within
the earth and at its mouth restores the sea.

How to Find the Animal Inside

Today I took a quiz,
one of those internet pseudo-scientific lists
that some fool thought up while snorting bath salts,
and found out my past life was spent roaming
among trees and rivers in the American West.

No, I was neither cowboy nor Indian.
As it turns out my personality evolved
from Canis lupus in various tell-tale ways.
I am swift, agile, and cunning. Well,
at least I'm a cunning linguist.

If you ignore the bad knees and arthritic hip,
one out of three ain't bad.
I value my family's well-being above all else.
That's true, but they refuse to believe it if I'm driving.
As far as being master of both day and night,

I nap well in darkness and light.
This quiz states that the wolf has a fiery temper,
which may explain my multiple marriages and a face
remodeled several times by knuckles. To be fair,
my father compared me more often to a catfish than a wolf.
He said, "You're all mouth and no brains."
Of all the answers given that prove my swap
from wolf to human, the most accurate is "not very social."
Ask a friend of mine, if you find one. I'd like to say
this self-examination, like my last testicular one, found no
abnormality or tragedy,
but the wolf may not agree.

Some Thoughts on Humility

1.

I never met Tim Hintz
but here's why I'd like to:
He worked the Gulf Coast waters
as a deep-sea diver, a world full
of rainbow-colored fish
and sunken Spanish treasure ships,
the place where a slight mistake
could end his life. That rush of risk
from blood to brain made every dive
a rebirth, a joy lost for me
as I sit at a desk from morning till night.
One day he packed away mask, flippers,
and the search for riches and moved
to Tennessee. Now, he builds
chairs from wood in the forest
near his new home, weaving
hickory bark gathered each spring
into seats that stretch across the red oak
frames and blue painted slots
he has cut and formed and hammered.
From the salt sea to a sea of trees,
he pursues the dance with each new step
while I struggle to walk.
I'd like to ask him what I've missed
confusing live with the word exist.

2.

I felt proud of my genius.
Lovers of my words bought me
drinks in gratitude as I regaled
crowded bars with platitudes
that shook the walls in brilliance.

I believed my soul to be immortal
because my poems were inspired.
Then, I cupped rain in my hands
during a summer shower and watched
as it leaked between my fingers,
swallowed by the unquenchable
thirst of the dry and unyielding earth.

3.

To Do:
Order cheap cigars
Feel guilty about ordering cheap cigars
Take dog to park
Read a Borges poem
Become an eternity within myself
Wash the car
Realize I was made of stardust
Wonder where stars come from
Take out the trash before my wife notices I haven't
Reheat leftover pizza for lunch
Worry how much more my arteries clogged after lunch
Nap just long enough not to dream
Exercise to extend lifespan lost by eating pizza
Revise mediocre novel
Increase its mediocrity
Make and drink one martini
Wish I drank more
Walk past a mirror and watch my smile mock me
Read someone else's famous mediocre novel
Remember to think of what is, not what if
Be jealous that an orchid wants only to be an orchid
Be thankful for darkness
Sleep

4.

My neighbor's porch leaned inward.
After his wife died,
rails
              collapsed,
The floor   stripped by termites,
steps
     rotted
           in the wet spring.
                         Still,
the damn thing won't fall down,
and it's fixable, like a flat tire,
a shattered window, or a bad haircut.
It takes time.
But, he never starts the work,
as if the effort's meaningless, as if
he knows that altering the present
will not correct the past, no matter
how much he wants to make it so.

5.

Today, my ex-wife bought
a pack of gum at the store
where I stopped for coffee.
Hiding behind the corn chips
and cupcakes like a shy teen
while the cashier rang her sale,
I felt embarrassed in the presence
of someone I had thought I loved.
Worn down by living, we never
sought to hurt each other. We
grew tired and then, apart.
She slipped from my grasp
as the rose petal does its calyx
when gravity is too much to bear.

6.

Twelve thousand feet:
the earth is veiled below
a translucent gauze
of smog and clouds.
Homes, like parade confetti,
line the curbed, browned
wheat fields.
The Wabash River
scrawls in looping letters
westward where it fuses
with a larger current
flowing south swallowed
by an ancient salt sea
to become full
by emptying,
to mourn
the loss of shadows
when the light goes out.

Tabla Rosa

my first philharmonic concert

Rain falls
but faster than rain.

A melody spreads like honey
                           leaking
over my blank mind.

Stars explode.
Their dust sifts through cello strings.

If life is melody willed by motion,
these walls breathe. They rise
and fall each time the conductor's arms flail the air
and resurrect the music Mozart died for.

If life is memory willed by senses,
I stand on Central Avenue in Jersey City
while its concrete fist unfurls in long fingers
of pool halls, warehouses and oyster bars.

                    I stare

upward at a window where lost love

gazes back.

If this concerto is a white rose

it blooms
      tonight,

a token of lost gardens planted
years before I knew
all things beautiful grow alone.

In its thorns earth fuses and forms
forests and mountains.
Through its petals dawn drains
moonlight from lakes and the wind
spins seasons into symphonies
authored by a single cell.

A Fisherman's Grace

The only time my Uncle Jim lost
his temper he had set down
his new tackle and lit a Lucky Strike.
The big snapping turtle
took the bait, the rod, the reel,
and all his composure, to the bottom.

The turtle never surfaced that day
but in the boat a sweat bee stung
me on the finger. I yelled
"fuck" for the first glorious time
just after my ears hooked
that word when it broke water, leaping
from Jim's lips—"Fuck, fuck,
oh fuck"—as he chased his sinking
tackle through the cattails
and then waded back to shore
like King Richard the Third,
a wet and winded shadow in the sunset.
Jim never spoke while he drove us home.

That night on the front porch, he danced by himself
as Benny Goodman's clarinet coaxed
"BlueRhapsody" out of the radio, and drank bourbon,
a whole quart. The more I watched him
the more the jazz came alive through
him, the notes got their melody
from the whisper of his shoes across the wooden floor.

When he finally passed out drunk
my mother laid gold cufflinks and a red tie
with his white shirt and blue Brooks Brothers suit.
"Your uncle would rather die than look too badly
dressed to enter the hospice in the morning," she said
as I helped her pack shaving cream, silk pajamas,
a Bass trophy, and his morphine pills.

Hop Along

for Tom

Phil thinks Hopalong Cassidy might have been God
reincarnated. Considering his point, I follow
his back down Bourbon Street, parting a curtain
of jasmine, sewage, bacon, and stale beer with my drunken body.
"This is the funk of life and bad love," he says,

but it's all too vivid for me, the smells, the embroidery cut
across Phil's western jacket and his long silver hair flashing
rainbows in the neon night. I can't help but wonder
why I'm here. What if all those evenings forty years ago
when old Hoppy galloped over the black & white TV screen

had passed me by as mere amusement and I missed some
apocryphal sign, some real second coming, returning now
to testify around the next corner on Rue Saint Ann?
If Hoppy and God were the same cowboy
then the existential dread riding herd on this outlaw
New Orleans night would simply be nothing.

Whew! It's only a mime who stands there and terrifies me
with gestures of a man imprisoned in a world he can't feel.
"I was Hopalong's stunt double once," says Phil. "I rode Topper
right off a goddamn cliff, then drowned. We all look like someone else
and you get a lot of pussy when you're a stunt man."

There's no one I can blame for Phil's brilliance or his 3-D
Technicolor cowboy boots as we cross Saint Ann and stop on Chartres
to ask for a table in the courtyard of the Napoleon House.
The bartender relives the history of Campari and swears
it's like life, never bitter if you add enough gin

and mix lime with the soda water. "Who would name a bar for a ghost
unless the ghost was a famous cowboy?" asks Phil.
Who would? And, looking over my shoulder, I wonder where

a mime might get off pretending he knows the secret of life is contained in a handful of air.

On Giving My Bicycle Away to a Charity

Mostly, the act was about the fear of falling.
I wanted to believe in the generous spirit
that helped a teen-aged boy bag groceries
at the market yesterday and brought my wife
a dozen roses instead of buying bourbon,
in the moral fiber that urged me to send
a wreath to the funeral home when
my neighbor died, even though he was
a prick, and volunteer at the food bank
during the last game of the World Series on TV.
The hope that I'm a better man than I am
spurs me onward in these charitable moments.
But what I think motivates me rarely does,
really. I've begun to grasp a more intimate
truth about humans in my twilight years.
Life is about not falling, especially as age
boosts the risk of harm. The road rises quickly
now to meet my wrinkled face, the asphalt
cuts deeper, and I bounce with less rebound
when a pot hole in the road brings me down.

The Garvin Gate Blues Festival in Louisville, Kentucky

1.

On the corner of Oak and Fourth
townhouses from a bygone era,
rusty red with age and hard use,
face the makeshift wooden bandstand.

In between music makers
and brick walls, the hot street shimmies
with strange remnants of a time
when even Baptists understood

harmony, rhythm and good wine,
not unlike the blood of Jesus,
covered a multitude of sins.
A plumber's shop, a Dollar Store,

the hair salon, and one old whore
stand unused, idled by the blues.

2.

There's one in every crowd
listening with his hands, convinced
that life has left him with fingers
to graft his soul into the sound,

grow beyond sums of frequency
and pitch or limits of an ear.
This man, lean and long, clicks two spoons
together on his dancing thigh

and levitates a bronzed woman
off the seat of her ten-speed bike.
Their bodies bend, loop, twist, and twirl
like winter wheat in a wind storm.

Entranced, they embrace the demon
in the boy drummer's voodoo snare.

3.

Debutantes from Anchorage,
the city's blueblood neighborhood,
seem frightened by a sax's wail
and the stench of poverty.

As they bravely tap a Gucci toe,
their faux-fur coats compliment
the booths of garish art and the smiles
painted on each junkie artist's face.

A dobro slides a lean row
of "Voodoo Queen" between
the earthy sound of horns and bass,
plowing toward the Delta from Chicago.

The whole crowd dreams in song,
hypnotized by song as dream.

4.

Before long, I wonder why I'm here,
bland and limp, like politicians
or spaghetti with no sauce, sharing
air burned by the scent of cheap wine

and the hint of antebellum angst
painted on these faces. A girl standing
on my right declares her pregnancy
through meth-stained teeth.

The father plays guitar onstage and wears
a hat that reads "Jesus is my boss."
What have I brought to offer back
the souls that gave me these words?

The exhalation of my own song,
a piece of my own death in strophes.

Polemics

Here's a mistake I frequently make,
I say poems are made from words.
But that is to say killing is an ordinary
task in war or all the tools for every job
come from Sears. Tonight, my poem
works as a bartender who, like an acrobat,
leaps on a narrow shelf. Steadied
by one leg and a waitress
with arms covered in pagan tattoos,
he retrieves a bottle high
above the bar's mirror breaking
neither neck nor sweat. Tonight
my poem is love as these two people
brush against each other and hesitate
till all that needs said is said in silence.
Leaves fall from trees constantly
without fearing death. The bartender
doesn't know this. That's why,
drying glasses with a damp towel, he looks
away each time she returns for an order.

August Blues on the River

My friend Rebe has a way
of making life seem pretty
great in these days
close to autumn
when fire in a cane break
would be a welcome relief
from the heat of an afternoon.
She told me soon I would see
Kaleidoscope skies,
smell the incense of things
dying only to be reborn.
She said, "Each year my sister
and her kiddos hand pick leaves
to send because they know
it's my favorite season."
Fall is their ritual of love,
prelude to a much needed rest
from the anger in summer
that burns time inward
until it's gone, like a candle
melts away its flame.
For an old man like me
autumn is a reminder
that to fear death is to suffer
the weight of living with no joy.
This was Rebe's message
sent in the simple gesture
of her nieces and carried by a trout
rising out of the water's current
in the oblique rays of sunset—
reds, blues, greens, and silver
blasting through the lax light
freed for a flash from the chains
of their own dark world.

A Change of Scenery

I'm weary
of steel and concrete
the cliched razor-edged
skyline reflected off
fluorescent lit glass,
of people with sharp edges
their conversations impossible
to separate from screeching
tires horns and construction,
of world class restaurants
with over-priced burgers,
long lines along a longer
row of brand name bargains,
and Broadway shows
too saccharine to pass for sugar.
I'm sad that each time I pass
a stray dog or his homeless friend,
dance with vacant-eyed junkies
around my bus stop who are
high on a gray-dawn swirl
of diesel fuel and meth,
I conjure colors I've lost
from falling leaves, smell
the fragrance of cedar pine
and honeysuckle vine,
and taste ancient forest oaks
braided with wild garlic
and thyme in the purple smog.

Climbing in the Garden of the Gods at Harrisburg, Illinois

Eons ago rain chiseled sandstone into something called Anvil Rock.
Now, I am here in this blink of a god's eye staring down the steep bluff,

searching for handholds on the way up from the forest below.
The more I search for truth outside myself the further it drifts away

like my father who backed two miles on a country road, gravel hurled
into space by the speed of whirring tires as he escaped a black cat

and yet, never outran his own shadow. Why do I think of dying
every time I'm happy? I'm a hundred feet up on this rock face.

The forest, smaller now, braids the scent of rain and pine around dirt
and moss rising from a damp stone handhold along the cliff wall.

Sweat cools my forehead like my mother's hand during a childhood fever.
Slipping on a rock, I learn how seconds fall away, where they go, when

time brings them to an end. This knowledge is useless to the storm
that brews above me, a turmoil more than time, more than flash and thunder,

more than a dog running off and howling in the wet wind.
It is the counterpoint harmony of an instant in a life and all of life at once,

the crystalline note that rises from the wind's fluid
strumming of tree limbs in sync with the drumming of my heart.

Interstate 24

I'm forty-nine miles from Chattanooga
stumbling through the radio in my pick-up truck
searching for noise to take away the ceaseless buzz
of tread bare Goodyear tires. Like a shark,
inertia drives me crazy. I decide a burred bearing
sounds better than Michael Buble & settle on a female
preacher who whines, "Beer is the real problem"
& I think of Jesus, his blanched bones scattered,
his soul in a make believe place, flesh desiccated
so our apathy matters. Jesus—wanting
only a draft or two of Pabst Blue after a hard day
with hammer & nails & blisters trying to carpenter
something solid, yet knowing nothing
of how to build paradise. Then, cousin John
coaxes him to a stream, holds his head under water,
deprives his brain of air till god appears as a dove.
That's when Jesus ends up hung on a stake
so the rest of us can feed on his misery
with our Inquisitions & Crusades, jihads & dead Jews,
televangelists who love meth & priests who love little boys.
Hell, we can't get ourselves born without originally sinning.
Then, a revelation comes in a blinding flash of lights
from a semi in the wrong lane, kinda like that time
when old apostle Paul fell off his ass on the road
to Damascus. Bang! This radio lady's bat-shit crazy
and no lady, beer ain't the "real" problem.

Addition

My friend Trish bears
a second beating heart.
It echoes
inside a room no man
can ever share.
Through a simple act
called sex, she became
a person who is
greater than the sum
of all her parts,
a goddess who creates
new life
with each contraction
of her own.

New Orleans Fais Do Do

Inside Poppy's Grill at 3:00AM, the thin cook
steams burgers beneath a chrome hubcap.
The scent of sausage grease and cayenne pepper
reminds me that hunger, of one kind or another,
always quickens my pulse.

A dark man, blind with bourbon, staggers
from the stool at the end of the counter
to an old fashioned jukebox, presses L-7
and plays a Clifton Chenier song.
His ink-colored eyes find a boy, who's dressed
like Marilyn Monroe, in the corner booth.
"Bon soir cher. Voulez-vous danser?"

The cook flips a burger. The dazed boy rises, hesitates
like the drop of sweat on the cook's left temple,
and falls into outstretched arms, a blonde rose petal
that has rejoined the flower.

Politely, his calloused Cajun leads. Two as one
they spin, sputter, and tilt around the dining area.
I clap, nod, stomp my foot and try to stay in time
till the motion makes me dizzy. Swirling
from the heat of cheap merlot, my appetite
merges with the dance, the soft flow of air lifting
the skirt, the damp panic pressed between their palms,
the slide of worn leather on sawdust, and the hint
of salt that mingles with hot flesh when strange lips meet.

Honestly

It is easy to feel sad
when you're old,
as Sisyphus must have

each evening for centuries
when he crested the hill.

With every passing day
friends' faces

fade quicker and a vague nausea
rises from the ancient warning
in a crow's cry.

This is natural
the experts say
for humans to concede
and fear mortality,
to realize that all you've done
and did not do will no longer
matter to anyone

but especially to you

and your flesh
will soon feed the earth.

Still,
think of the tired god's joy
to wake each morning
and find the stone
at the bottom again.

Peeling Potatoes

Numbness sprouts in fingertips and crawls up the forearm,
a Wandering Jew of monotonous veins, into the neck,
over the brain until you don't remember what you're doing, or why,
only that the task must be completed before synapses choke
the last few bored cells to death and all that remains is a scream.
This is similar to shopping at Wal-Mart or telemarketing.
You've done both in times of great personal crisis.
Once, when it seemed that your prostate had swollen
from lack of use, you did them together careening a crippled metal
shopping cart between rows of mouthwash and calamine lotion,
past bags of peat moss and fishing gear, motor oil and paper towels,
Timex watches and semi-precious wedding rings, across deserts
of ugly shirts and cat litter, talking all the time to a guy named Bill
on the cell phone about a free vacation at Disney World.

Sometimes, potato peelings clog the drain and things get thorny.
Your wife yells from the bedroom, "Call the plumber." "I'll do it
myself," you say, and then scrounge a drain snake from a neighbor,
with his assurance the springy rod will cure any problem in five minutes.
Two hours later, soaked in sewage from the overflowing sink,
you drive to Wal-Mart and search for Draino and a set of earplugs,
all the while listening long distance on your new Apple iPhone
to the meaning of life as a salesman from Bombay tries to sell
you new tires for a golf cart you don't own.

Back at home, the mother-in-law sits in the kitchen,
reminding the wife about the doctor she could have married, if only
she would have stayed in nursing school and not gained the extra weight.
You return to peeling potatoes, this time over a trash can where the brown rinds
spiral down and cover the refuse of life—coffee grounds, milk cartons,
newspapers, beer cans (you don't recycle), fish wrappers, tin foil, yogurt cups,
cereal boxes, a pack of Camels (you quit yesterday, but may dig them out soon),
a letter from Publisher's Clearing House saying you've won.
Suddenly, you remember Charles Simic's famous poem about shrimps
and wonder why you aren't smart enough to understand its deeper meaning.
Your wife and her mother grow silent until the paring knife slips,

sliding through skin on the right thumb as if it were a sauteed onion slice. "Don't bleed on the floor. The dog will lick it up," they both say in unison. Rinsing that thumb, you decide at last these spuds being slaughtered are dreams trying not to die, wounded with water, starch, and dirt, struggling to keep their skin, and then, diced to satisfy someone else's hunger.

How We Were What We Never Became

I'm trying to write a poem about how we saved America,
Baby Boomers, born from the ashes of the second World War
when our fathers came back from saving America from the first
one that promised to be "a war that ended all war."
We were magic—all wind and fire, red blood and thunder,
freedom and love—as we embraced the paradise in our grasp.
I've written several lines already and then scratched through
them with a force that caused me to replace my felt pen.
Half phrases about social conscience, electric guitars, LSD,
equality, and a vague thought from Borges about memory
keeping images sacred grace the page and die there for want
of fresh air, for the same lack of purpose that kills every dream.
That's when I realized that Borges may have been wrong.
Images keep memories sacred. Around my room icons rest
within my view that remind me of the holy moments in my life,
especially the conch shell rescued from Rye Beach during some
rock concert in 1969 that failed to bring world peace. I still raise
it to my ear all these decades later and listen as the ocean's waves
roar within its hollow center, and the magic changes nothing.

Naturally Unnatural

The doctor said my impotence was "organic" in origin
and after perusing both meanings of the word, I'm left
with a medical opinion that he must have been mistaken.

Of course, he's correct in assuming:
My penis works as a reproductive, intromit organ that additionally
serves as the urinal duct, blah, blah, blah—what fool doesn't know that?
But, quite remiss by assuming that:
> The nature of my affliction is drawn from living matter, or arises from
> matters of living as if it were an STD.
The possibilities are infinite and almost always concerned with more
> ephemeral and often inorganic circumstance.

For example:
> Wading in rice paddies irrigated with Agent Orange
> Bourbon induced euphoria to forget said rice paddies
> Failure in discerning the meaning of love
> A bad haircut
> The paradox of dominion over earth and insignificance to a tree
> Blindness that accompanies seeing too much
> The absolute truth that nothing is absolute
> An awareness that metaphor has no value apart from function
> Ed egli avea del cul fatto trombelta

> Etc. Etc. Etc.

Sonnet of True Love

We hid beneath a row of rose bushes,
neatly trimmed, ready to bloom
and so were those bushes. The sky
was high and bright, our parents
gone to work and the sitter
somewhere in a gloomy room
reading *Life Magazine* to herself.
Gnats attacked our sweaty tomb.

"Show me yours first," Martha said.
I did, a fat, tiny grub worm of a thing
without a hood, slick and single-eyed
as I was years away from pubic hair.
Her laughter proved a true reply
for all my lack of s'avoire faire.

Poem About Writing a Novel

Every morning I sit at my desk and think about writing
the great American Novel, not the ones that Wal-Mart sells
or drugstores place on swirling metal racks, not *Fifty Shades*
of anything or with a protagonist private detective, especially
no ghost-written sci-fi apocalypse or daddy-diddled me thriller,
but rather a simple story that may benefit future generations
if we decide again to ever teach children to read more than
a sound-byte on a gray screen.

I'd like my novel to be chock full of leitmotifs and metaphors
with characters that develop and a plot unafraid to complicate.

It's possible that my novel will contain some mystery, perhaps
a snowstorm in the summer or a woman who looks like Jesus.

In keeping with contemporary and mostly postmodern rules,
the hero may be male or female or a combination thereof,
short or tall, thin or fat with some low self-esteem issues,
and born into any race so long as I don't appropriate culture
from one other than my own.

My novel will go on and on for several hundred pages appearing
as a slice of ordinary life, but with a dark resonance that may never
be fully understood, just as my own life, by neither reader nor me.
After a long struggle, the book will win some sort of prize
and be published to critical acclaim. Sales will falter quickly to mark
its brilliance and I will be forced by poverty to work as a teacher
in some prestigious program for young writers of mediocre talent
until death brings me the fame I deserve.

The Continuous Positive Airway Pressure Machine

It has always seemed odd to me that sleep,
a process meant to restore life—muscles,
blood, bone, and brain—to its former glory
should mirror perfectly
the ineluctable finality of death.

Yet, my doctor believes I have something
called apnea, which means I quit breathing
several times every hour even if dreaming
of naked women bronzed by sun, sensuous
with sweat and playing volleyball on a beach.
Here I am sipping a Mai-Tai as they bounce by
and in reality, I'm dead.

This painless marvel occurs
for many reasons, not the least of which
seems to be my body fat and leaves me
minus something I can't live without.
Just when I reach the point of extinction
my medulla whispers, "Not tonight buster."

The cure was simple and of double use,
a mask that forces me to breath
with no funereal interruption and requires
no effort on my part to hide my face,
a trick that exhausts me in the light of day.

Smoker's Wake

We earned manhood in the boxing ring,
my brother and I, at summer camp,
pimpled boys spurred on by dreams
of sexual exploits from the girls' cabins
across the clearing. In those days the danger

of speaking to a female far outweighed
a broken nose or bruised ego suffered
at the sharp right hook of some country boy
the same size and burdened with the same
lack of social grace we possessed.

The camp director called three minute
bouts "smokers" but never told us why
since none of us were at the age
of twelve. We guessed it had to do
with the flaming swiftness of our punches

and ashes left in their wake. We were wrong,
of course. It had more to do with ragged breath,
nausea, sweat, and the weakness in our achy knees
as the leather of the gloves felt like lead and each
punch grew shorter toward the end of every round.

Who knew at our age life would be exhausting?
We sensed no problems, no gender need or holy rite
to knock an opponent on his ass, only chaos that felt
immortal, a trick in our minds, a craving in the body
that would one day leave the world in ruin.

National Anthem

David writes the President once a month
ever since he walked, stoned outta his gourd, off Khe Sahn.
Swear-to-God, once every month, no matter who's President.

He hopes someone in the White House might remember
what could have been had we not stumbled on our own cliches,

trading handmade tie-dyes for MTV stock, swapping
vinyl records and beer bottles that pry open, for IPods, Blue Rays,
anthrax in the mail and malt beverages flavored with exotic fruits.

He chooses to ignore why we deal conscience,
like scrap metal, for corporate logos and Kalashnikov's.

Instead, David asks the President to replace
our Star-Spangled Banner with "Sugar Magnolia" and have
a marble statue of Jerry Garcia sculpted for the Rose Garden,

painted black and back-lit with a neon bulb flashing
—Gratefully Dead—twenty-four hours a day.

Out of Focus

In '69, I met a wild-haired man named Reggie
who walked an empty dog collar on a stiff leash,
who prowled the savage island between adolescence and adulthood,
popping Dexedrine, swilling Ripple, talking baby talk
to the dog collar. "Gude poochie. Poochie poochie hoochie coo."
The first time I saw his paralyzed smile, we smoked black hash
laced with white veins of opium. Our feral eyes drifted with the smoke,
unmoored skiffs in a current of cold light.
I got a hard on when Reggie's girl rubbed her breasts
across my arm and asked for the last toke.
I passed the pipe, but Reggie stood there frowning
and sucking air as the water pipe bubbled.
The strange girl giggled "All gone." Reggie's right foot
pounded the pavement and he sang along with a John Lee Hooker 8 track,
"I'm your poochie poochie man. Everybody knows I am."
His voice squealed like sneakers on a clean gym floor.
When the tape ended, Reggie turned his collar up, petted the air,
and walked slowly into the night.
He's a chemist now, hired by Bristol Myers
because of his phenomenal pharmaceutical knowledge
and I'm a poet, drunk on words, stumbling over
the illusion of art.
For forty years we've brushed our wild hair away.
He helped develop Prozac too late to save his own brittle grin
or my last few healthy brain cells;
but the man still walks an empty dog collar late at night.
He just bought the John Lee Hooker box set on CD.
Some evenings we sit together on a park bench, smoking dope
until the moon changes colors and the dog collar pisses on my leg.

The Changing Rain

It happens before you
even notice how wet this one
afternoon has become.
The earth around you shivers
and the air smells sadder. Trees
appear thinner, more hungry
in the shadows of an earlier dusk.
By tomorrow, the wind will be
twenty degrees colder
and autumn will have ended.
Your knee will ache.
You will sleep less and less
in the nights that follow.
Lines between dreams
and thoughts begin to blur
even in the warm womb
of an extra blanket.
You have been through
this shift in seasons
for many decades, but lately
you are filled with wonder
at how easily you missed
the press of time with each.

Vision Problems

As a child, I never saw my father
less than perfect even when he drank
or sensed my mother lonely as she sat
for hours reading romance novels
until the day she died.
I fell in love with a woman who was
not the woman I fell in love with.
In Vietnam, I viewed war as a path to peace,
the growl of guns and the howl of bombs
the symphony of its serenity.

Today, a man named Mark euthanized
my sweet dog, Dallas. It was his only job.
He scowled constantly.
Tattoos ran the length of both arms,
multi-colored demons and angels
with wings for ears.

He laid her on a table,
his voice as soft as a spring rain
on a sun-scorched day, inconsistent
with the cruel crook of his thick lips
and the kink in his once-broken nose.
Her eyes closed, relieved as the injection
stopped her heart. Ours eyes welled in tears
and Mark spoke the final words she heard,
"It's the last best thing we do for them."

On the ride home, I thought of my mother
who wasted away years ago, a lingering
torment caused by some vague notion
about the "sanctity" of life conveyed to us
by her doctor and her priest.
I remember her eyes as we fed her paste
through a hole in her stomach, searching
an empty sky through the window for angel

or demon, like the ones pictured on Mark,
to release what little was left of a soul,
and I wish I'd seen his wisdom then.

The Garden

for my wife, Debbi

                Remember ours?

How we turned the earth over, rubbed the sore soil
with a poultice of eggshells and Miracle Gro
as if it were our stung and fevered child. We covered
seeds, hoed unwanted weeds, exorcized crows
and rabbits in a strange ritual of dance and song.
Until that summer, our neighbors never heard
"Appalachian Spring" played on pots and pans
by a tattooed drunk twirling spoons.

When the corn grew straight and the staked tomatoes
rounded with red life and the squash leaked upward,
our laughter sprayed them all with light. There was no sadness,
only the salmon color of sunrise and a frenzied desire
to wade barefoot in the dew.

                Remember the storm?

Around here hog farmers, grain haulers, and old women
still call these small twisters Fingers of God because
even a slight touch drives shafts of straw into oak trees
like ten penny nails, houses explode, trains
writhe like garter snakes, airborne. People become memories,
like my father's sister, buried beneath joists, broken beams
and the expectations of her parents.

You cried for hours over the tangled stalks and shattered vines,
cursed all gods for having fingers that would reach down
and rip a dream from someone sustained by little else,
then rented a small plow and returned the earth to a black void
till spring and your strength came again. I laughed
and bought fresh produce at Conway's Market, not grasping,
that our garden was never about the crop.

Tune-Up

The man who fixes my car
came from Jordan,
doesn't drink booze,
fasts during Ramadan, and
never built a bomb.

The only terrorists he knows are his small children
who behave much the same as mine did at an early age
and a wife that makes him scrub grease from under
his nails before daring to sit down to dinner.

He treats me fair,
does good work,
has never overcharged
anyone I know
for his labor.

I would not kill this man for any god and do not fear
for my life when the oil gets changed in my Ford. I call
him friend and might even loan him money, if I had some.
He would not send a drone to my daughter's wedding.

Measuring

1.

Bobby drew a circle in the red dirt.
We opened our tobacco pouches—mine was
a blue Bugler emptied by my chain-smoking
uncle Jim—and poured glass marbles
onto the ground. They were cool to touch,
liquid, and in the sunlight flashed
like an early morning frost. It was recess
at Lowell School. Around us other students
squealed, laughed, leapt over jump ropes,
and spun on the broken merry-go-round
as it wobbled like a weakening top.
The teacher's cheap perfume twirled about
the scent of cut grass. We had no fear
of the future, neither Bobby nor I, no desire
beyond the pure joy of listening to the click
and clack rhythm of the sparkling spheres as
they fell within the boundaries of the game.
Bobby won first shot by virtue of a cat's eye.
He laid a marble on his thumb and flicked
it at my favorite green one. The marble rolled
across the dirt and nudged mine over the line.
It was the first time I learned that hunger
comes from loss, but not the last.

2.

My mother left me her can opener.
It's electric and she's been dead for twenty years.
I use it every day and can't imagine it broken,
tired, or sick and that's the good and bad
about simple machines. They never quit working
even when we do. No one worships
their creators or prays for them to end suffering.
It's an irony not lost on the wise among us.

3.

The fear of not knowing
drives me to despair today
and the horror lies in
not knowing what it is
I'm supposed to know,
like a child at a market
who runs up and down
each aisle and searches
for an answer to hunger
he does understand
or the hunter's shadow
that stalks the trail
of a deer without a why.

4.

In the lobby of the Premier Car Wash
while I pay five white Christian kids
from northern Georgia a few dollars
to scrub my car, I'm thinking about
the wild-eyed man from the church
twenty-six miles down the road,
how he stood last Sunday as the pastor
chose to honor school teachers in his sermon.
Shouting "Don't let Satan educate
your children," he fired his middle finger
toward the forlorn Jesus replica that hung
on a plastic cross above the pulpit.
Of course, the police arrested him
for his outburst as a sinner of small
proportions and later let him go
with a fine and the promise of silence.

5.

I am a man whose life has been worn away
by time, and yet lucky on certain mornings
to be filled with a mysterious sort of wonder
in the pit of my stomach, as if I had driven
over a hill too fast or heard the wind speak
my name in the instant before a rain storm.

I am a man who sees the outline
of mountains through the thin film
of a grey fog along the Blue Ridge trail,
smells the rebirth of spring in silt and fish
and decayed earth along the river's edge,
hear the veil of holy silence lift in the choir

of cardinals, blue jays, sparrows, Carolina
wrens and the screech of a red-tailed hawk,
decodes the cryptic rattle of squirrels skittering
through the Georgia pines, balances one foot
at a time on the stones that split the current
as the water sculpts a million-year-old shrine.

I am a man lost in a labyrinth of laughter
blooming around my legs—snap dragons,
wild strawberries, peonies beneath a pine tree,
lilies of the valley, bleeding hearts
dandelions—and each step I take scatters
seeds for butterflies that flash like shooting stars.

Here an ancient turtle crosses my path,
its journey undeterred by fear of what lay ahead.

6.

My wife
feeds the fishes
in our farm pond each day

with bits of cheese, rabbit pellets,
or bread crumbs from the last of a stale loaf.

They rise
to greet her shadow
like fat water lilies
as the sun warms the surface of the water.

These fish
do not know, or maybe
do not care, that soon she will attach
their cornucopia of goodness to a barbed hook
and pull them
into a foreign world
where they will slowly drown.

7.

I only know
what I know
If I knew
what I thought
I knew
I'd know
a lot more
than I know now.

8.

The dog ignores every word I say,
especially "please don't do that"
no matter if she's rips furniture,
chases squirrels into the street,
roots around the trash, or terrifies
the post man. I paid a thousand
dollars to a canine expert for her
to learn restraint based on respect
for my voice. He came highly

recommended, although
not by other dogs.

Alter Idem

A poetry reading in the Balkans after the war

We stood
one at a time
in various stages
of composition,
chanting
wild vowels
and consonants
as if the same
wool blanket woven
from different
languages might warm
us all, as if
smoke rising
in the room
might mingle
somewhere over
our heads,
signal us into the past
and remind us
that a few paved miles
ringed by mountains
were once all we had
between us,
not the ocean
of rhetoric
or the demagogues
that waged the wars,
or leftover landmines
that rip the legs and arms
from future generations
who may never
understand:
the first walls that must
come down

are ones bricked
with words.

Snapshots

I wish I were a camera. I wish it all the time.
My eyes would have a reason, my life would have a rhyme.
—David Crosby

1—1/5/56

How big Aunt Betty's belly
looked when I was eight years old,
how she cried and vomited every morning
for months, even after Doc Peck said,
"There's nothing there but hysteria."
Still, my mother held a cold cloth
to her sister's forehead with one hand,
pretending to feel the baby move with the other.

2—1/5/67

Monsoons shot raindrops bigger
than bullets. They strafed my helmet,
a symphony of sameness, a hypnotic
splattered mist that never lifted.
In the bunker I dreamt dry dreams
of Saigon streets—the sway
of rickshaws, rattle of palm trees,
the rustle of silk, the adrenalin
tingling in a French whore,
and defeated the desire to lie face down
in the bright yellow mud, just one more
casualty of a constant dull thud.

3—1/5/68

My fireteam eased by a thatch hut, palms sweating,
safeties off, frightened boys on a first dance

with the dying. A widow squatted in the webbed shadows
and picked through a child's matted hair. Her fingers
pulled lice from the scalp. She bit the heads off, one at a time,
while I imagined my body twitching between uneven teeth,
tumbling through betel juice and drool to the dead ground.
That night, alone in my bunker, away from her eyes, I stared
as orange and blue flames from a smudge pot waltzed black
shadows across the sandbags. Even in the uncertain light,
I never lost my focus as a soldier. Even in the soft rustle
of diesel smoke, I never cared why she was a widow.

4—1/5/78

Today, four sparrows flew as one bird
from a black bridge railing on the Wabash River.
A fisherman floating beneath me unfolded
his nylon net, feeding the caramel water dreams
of a big catch, while the wind brayed at his back.
He stood in the bow swaying like an unsteady drunk
on an uneven dance floor and waved as if we were
friends. As if we were friends, I waved back.

5—1/5/88

My cup left a ring of spilled coffee
on the table. Each time I drank and returned
the cup, the circle became less whole,
rearranged constantly by pressure from a source
it could not recognize. On my plate, two
poached eggs stared upward. I felt the increasing weight
of unbuttered toast in my hand and the slight flutter
of a sparrow's wing in my chest.

6—1/5/90

Everything was white, except the blood
and my son's ceramic eyes. How big they looked
for an eight year old, like blueberries
in small bowls of milk. Outside the window,
beyond the smell of isopropyl, white snow
strangled the frightened trees. John's surgeon said,
"The tumor's gone, we think. Nothing but air now."
I held a cold cloth to my son's forehead with one hand,
pretending to feel the empty space with the other.

7—1/5/2000

From the top of the Farm Bureau Co-op
grain elevator, I see the dead tree
in the yielding meadow beyond Lynch Road
where Mike pissed twice on prom night before
lightning split the wood and chased
us along the ground, as if it were a hot yellow stream the sky
pissed back. Mike outran that lightning
till it caught him on a jungle trail outside Phu Bai.
I'm still running.

Epilogue

Dia de los Muertos

The First Death

When I die, I will be saved from death
by Mexicans. Each November strangers
who never saw me trip and tumble
over a crack in the sidewalk, heard me
curse another drunk on a crowded street,
smelled my cheap cigars, or touched
my scarred body, will eat candy skulls
and drink martinis in my honor.
Senoras with rich black hair, who never
spoke with my ex-wives, will light copal
to ward off evil and then dance in my honor,
arms flailing like flowering vines
in the midnight wind, bodies shivering
at the hips in anticipation that I might
bring them something more than love,
like Roceria did as she swayed
in the bow of Miguel's boat
that one summer so long ago when I drove
to Acapulco and dove for conch shells.
Children will place the petals of orange
marigolds along a path from Saltillo
to Indiana that I may find my way back
to some sacred space they have reserved
for me where no senses are censured on the day
of the dead, except those most important,
the chance to feel once more, hot blood
drummed through pulsing veins and to gaze
with depth and weight into the eyes of love,
to have the space I fill regain its meaning.

The Second Death

Hushed and solemn
voices will lower me past their black suits
into a world where mud is my only sky
and the earth holds me close like a mother might
clutch a soldier finally come home from war.
Out of my sight, their words will echo as laughter
at the end of a hollow pipe. They will smoke
cigarettes, toss roses on the loose dirt,
remind themselves of the time I saved a baby
from a burning building, carried my last cup
of water to a thirsty nun, gave someone
the shirt off my back, donated kidneys and lungs,
hearts and livers to the sick, bathed lepers
and, if not for my lust for women, might
have become pope. I would like to remain
in this limbo each November when boundaries
relax between their world and my dead one.
I am a better man where memory meets fantasy.

The Final Death

Memory is the devil that owns my soul
and when those who remember me die,
I will be put to rest.
On that day, no one lights incense for me.
Those left to drink and dance rejoice
for different ghosts who still take form
in the shadowed doorways of the mind.
On that day I will become the starling
I saw last winter trapped behind a great
window in the library where I sat
reading poems. The bird beat itself
senseless against the glass. Free space
trapped inside the frenzy of unattainable
flight drove it crazy until an old man
I didn't know threw a towel over its head,
lifted it gently and carried it out of sight.

Epitaph

My friend Ken studied philosophy,
read all the great masters and claimed
no stone could skip the surface of any lake
and not leave lasting evidence of its existence.

Critics on Jim McGarrah's Poetry

Jim McGarrah's debut, *Running the Voodoo Down*, is a book of intense, highly crafted, and haunting poems in the voice of a wild man shouting unflinching truth about the congested speedway of contemporary living he is roaring through. And what's better is the poetry is equal to the richness of the life led.

—Jack Myers, Texas Poet Laureate, 2003

In Jim McGarrah's third poetry collection, the present is often eclipsed by the ghosted past of Vietnam. These vital poems dwell in the inevitable privacy of being human, and it is in these starkly singular spaces--walking the dog, truckstopping for breakfast, closing the bar at 2 am, visiting Vietnamese children suffering the effects of Agent Orange-that McGarrah wrestles truth with music, grit and wry humor. As the poet sways between sobriety and stupor, bearing witness to the horror of being alive and the horror of going on, he too leads us through that slim midnight portal into rugged grace, where a worn ball cap becomes a whiskey-washed Eucharist and the cast of the missing creates the genius of absence. When transcendence comes, it is no lavish exaltation, but something far more real and astonishing.

—Jennifer K. Sweeney, author of *How to Live on Bread and Music*, winner of the James Laughlin Prize

Jim McGarrah knows the back roads of the American Psyche and the kind of solar flares the brain releases when you pull off the electro-throb highway and smell the real people. Like Wim Wenders' angels he listens to the inner plaints and pleas beneath the noise of everyday life. He hears the old woman, Marge, who says that we are all "Collateral damage in God's plan" and Jesus, the carpenter with blistered hands, who downs a cold one at the bar. Reading this book is like coming home.

—Doug Anderson, author of *The Moon Reflected Fire* and winner of the Kate Tufts Discovery Prize

www.ingramcontent.com/pod-product-compliance
Lightning Source LLC
Chambersburg PA
CBHW020930090426
42736CB00010B/1101